Multi-Family Housing
The Art of Sharing

Multi-Family Housing

The Art of Sharing

Michael J. Crosbie

Published in Australia in 2003 by
The Images Publishing Group Pty Ltd
ACN 059 734 431
6 Bastow Place, Mulgrave, Victoria 3170, Australia
Telephone (61 3) 9561 5544 Facsimile (61 3) 9561 4860
E-mail: books@images.com.au
Website: www.imagespublishinggroup.com

ISBN: 1 87690 769 X

Coordinating Editor: Fiona Gruber
Designed by The Graphic Image Studio Pty Ltd, Mulgrave, Australia
Film separations by Fine Arts Repro House Co., Ltd.
Printed by Sing Cheong Printing Co. Ltd. Hong Kong.

CONTENTS

AUTHOR'S PREFACE

During an interview I conducted with Robert Venturi a few years ago, I asked what was the most complicated building he had ever been asked to design—knowing that he had worked on laboratories, fire stations, museums, and the like. He immediately answered, "a house." I was surprised by the answer. Surely a house couldn't be that complex, not as demanding as a lab. Venturi pointed out that a house was more than the fulfillment of a program. Rather, it was (or could be) the very reflection of the people who lived there—the public face of the private lives of those who dwelled within.

How much more complex, then, is multifamily housing. For in this building type we have the psychological and social demands of the single-family home plus the accommodation of families living together—families of all shapes and sizes. Multifamily housing must satisfy the human need for self-expression in built form (which single-family homes more easily accommodate) yet also foster a sense of community. Such projects are delicate balances of public face and private spirit, individual space and communal identity.

The projects in this book fulfill these demands in varying degrees, given their programs and locations. In large-scale multifamily housing projects, it is sometimes difficult to accommodate both public roles and private needs. In a project such as The Siena in New York, the scales are tipped more in the direction of public role. This 31-story residential building is designed first and foremost to respond to its midtown Manhattan site, and to fulfill its civic architectural duties. Its exterior is a reflection of its proximity to the landmark church, St. Jean Baptiste Eglise, and its rectory. It must also acknowledge its place in the city, and in so doing sacrifices the possibility of individual expression of the residents. Yet, as an urban home, it meets the desire of many city dwellers to command an impressive address.

In another example of city living, the Twenty Niagra project in Toronto manages to express the notion of an "individual home" within its urban context, facing a municipal park. Here, the units are expressed on the exterior primarily through views in and views out. The multistory apartment spaces are capable of being read from the exterior through large expanses of glazing and private terraces or balconies, many of which look out over the park.

Creating community in urban density is no easy task. A new project inserted into an established urban context must make connections with the flow of life around it. A good example of this is the Mockingbird Station project in Dallas. The loft apartments are designed to express the vibrancy of living at the very center of this college community. In fact, many of the units overlook the Mockingbird rail station, which is a constant reminder of the stream of commuters and residents that give this neighborhood its energy. Locating the units on the upper stories, above the hum, where residents can observe yet be part of this communal scene, stitches this multifamily housing project into the urban life that surrounds it.

Recognizing the history of the neighborhood in which one builds distinguishes several of the projects in this book. Perhaps one of the strongest and most comfortable is Ellen Wilson Place in Washington, D.C. Here the size, scale, and form of city dwellings built a century or more ago is honored without devolving into a thin pastiche. The materials, details, and building traditions of the surrounding context were carefully studied, and the architect introduced modified housing forms while making sure that the new building felt "at home." Color, texture, and decorative details help tie the new buildings into the old neighborhood, while the architectural variety lends a sense that these homes have been built over time. In all, according to the architect, 36 different façade designs and five different building types "evoke the sporadic and staccato rhythms" of the setting, reinforced with the use of 22 different bricks, 17 mortar colors, eight window colors for 30 window sizes, and 15 ornamental stair-railing designs.

History can be summoned in other ways, for other purposes. In Puyallup, Washington, for instance, the Silvercrest Senior Housing project is home to a large number of Scandinavian immigrants. Bright yellow, red, and green on the exterior suggest the decorative exuberance of Scandinavian farm buildings, while Silvercrest's atmosphere of a large, friendly lodge helps to make it fit with nearby single-family homes.

According to an ancient Persian proverb, "When a man's house ceases to be built, he dies." A more eloquent expression of the connection between our lives and the sustaining nature of our homes would be hard to find. The very expression of this life-giving force is best seen in the Bay Bridge project in Oakland, California. This is a project that met stiff neighborhood resistance (housing for lower-income singles with AIDS) on an inhospitable site (facing a freeway off-ramp). Not only did the architect (Michael Pyatok, who wrote this book's Introduction) create a sensitively scaled and communal project: he also affirmed the lives of the residents by introducing a "living wall," covered with vines and inset with bright red birdhouses that he donated to encourage new life to take up residence.

This project and many others in this book balance with great acumen the need for multifamily housing to reflect the hopes and dreams of the residents and to nurture a shared community.

Michael J. Crosbie
Essex, Connecticut

INTRODUCTION

MULTIFAMILY HOUSING DESIGN IN THE 21ST CENTURY

The production of housing is an integral part of American culture, reflecting all of its social, economic and political complexities as they vary from region to region. This rich texture of the U.S. cultural landscape is probably the reason its housing industry has never succeeded in establishing a system of centralized production. Housing production in the U.S. is highly fragmented among about 55,000 builder/developers, of whom nearly 80 percent produce less than 20 units a year, according to the U.S. Department of Housing and Urban Development. Some see this as inefficient, with production each year falling behind the growing need. Others see fragmentation as a blessing, possessing the potential to respond to the unique mixture of local demographic preferences, history, climate, and available labor and material resources.

Others may argue that "inefficient" production leading to a shortfall of housing is a matter of political perspective. To this view, each year America produces more than enough housing for its citizens, at least in square footage, but with too many receiving homes of 10,000 square feet or more, and too many receiving too little to meet their needs, and some receiving none at all, according to HUD. The problem is not that we under-produce, it is that we unevenly distribute what we produce, because housing production occurs within a market economy notorious for not achieving an equitable distribution of resources. So housing production is a sociopolitical enterprise with all of its attending frictions, whether in inner cities with gentrification caused in part by returning wealth, or in suburbs with environmental and agricultural degradation resulting from ever-expanding circles of wealth on-the-run.

The recent affliction of SUVs (sports utility vehicles) in personalized transportation has been accompanied, if not preceded, by the "SUV-ization" of homes like mega-houses, of retail outlets like Walmart, and now even of art museums like the Guggenheim's proposal for a site on Manhattan's East River. Our patterns of consumption, settlement, transportation, and habitation are intertwined with the poverty of other nations. Until we as a nation experience the daily pinch of limited resources like most of the rest of humanity, whose resources and labor we have been exploiting, we will not understand why we are so despised as a nation, and why the days of our present lifestyle are finite.

ARCHITECTS AND HOUSING DESIGN

Architects and their various design ideologies are deeply embedded in these patterns of housing production and consumption. The pursuit of superficial fashion and useless novelty is the cultural justification for unending consumption in market economies, and the architectural profession has not been immune to this tendency. Sponsors of high profile cultural or commercial symbols, working with budgets freed from the worries of rigorous financial feasibility, nearly always encountered by multifamily housing, often tolerate and encourage a whimsical pursuit of novelty to attract attention. These trophy buildings make architecture extremely vulnerable to the pursuit of novelty for its own sake and encourage its practice to weave itself into a seamless union with the fashion industry.

In the housing industry, custom homes for the wealthy often share the budgetary freedom of high-profile trophy buildings, and often qualify as "real architecture" as defined by today's fashion industry. On the other hand, the requirements of multifamily housing thrust architects deeply into the sociopolitical and economic malaise outlined above. Budgets are rarely "fat," except for high-density luxury living, so exotic novelty is a privilege for only a few. High-end trophy buildings for commercial or cultural purposes may occasionally cause a cultural teapot tempest in their pursuit of fashionable novelty. But the design of whole new communities on the urban edge or the transformation of existing ones near the urban center can stir up many environmental and class conflicts, if not race and ethnic frictions, that reach regional if not national proportions. Faced with this level of potential resistance, no wonder then that multifamily housing is often accused of being too conservative by the design subculture.

So whether architects like it or not, multifamily housing, along with its frequent companion of community or neighborhood planning, often forces them to confront many of our society's most pressing problems. From the viewpoint of a practitioner, I see these classified as environmental, cultural, social and economic, and only lastly, technological.

ENVIRONMENTAL ISSUES

Multifamily housing, by its sheer size and impact, often consumes land and material resources in quantities that people perceive as large when compared to other additions to their communities. While not necessarily approaching the perceived impacts of highways, shopping centers, or big-box retail, they can stir emotions when former open spaces begin to shrink or other cherished natural or revered resources seem to be threatened. Too much of post-World War II sprawl has justified the public's fear of new developments. But even in this day, protests are intense when more enlightened developments build closer to existing infrastructure, in more compact patterns, preserve and restore wetlands and other natural conditions, or attempt to be "green," and even seek to introduce and support public transit. While sometimes justified, the resistance too often seems selfishly focussed on preserving existing conditions for those now living in the contested location. Americans cherish expanding their families, but too often are unwilling or unable to make the connection between the growth required in their communities and the offspring that they are producing in their own bedrooms.

Under these circumstances, architects, landscape architects, land planners, and their developer-clients must work miracles with designs that are more sensitive to environmental and historic conditions. Their work must be guided by informed, careful political maneuvering, and hopefully, by sincere public education campaigns and participatory design processes that genuinely incorporate public opinion while at the same time informing it. When dealt with openly and honestly, people can become wiser and more generous, both to the environment and the needs of each emerging generation looking for places to live. Architects need to be critical players in that education process, both in the design and planning phase, and in the quality of the resulting product, which while in use continues that public education process for years afterwards.

CULTURAL ISSUES

It is our fate as humans to develop irrational attachments to places, and quite often communities have formed in places where humans should never have settled, resulting in self-destructive patterns from a sustainable perspective. Yet generations have made these places home, leaving behind buildings and places that become endeared symbols of theirs and their ancestors' aspirations and dreams. These are realities that developers and their design teams cannot ignore when designing to suit the images of domesticity and the sense of history that intangibly combine in a region's memories and built forms. Avant-garde experiments in novelty for its own sake when applied to multifamily housing succumb to the pressures of mainstream design publications. When inserted into the complex cultural conditions of an existing community they can often cause a hatred for more compact, higher density, and income-diverse developments, so necessary for saving a region's natural and cultural heritage.

As long as multifamily housing designers recognize that their larger mission is to convince people that they should be living at higher densities, with mass transit, in smaller dwellings and in mixed-use/mixed-income communities to conserve land, energy, and resources, and maybe even bridge some class and race divides, then they should have no guilt for eschewing avant-garde fashion in order to accomplish these longer-term and more radical contributions to social change. Designing imagery to help induce structural changes in the culture that will prolong the life of the planet for everyone, far outweighs the short-term purposes of using design to change consumer preferences toward superficial appearances cherished by the design subculture and fashion industry.

Once again, as with the environmental issues, design teams must recognize that community design is an intense cultural enterprise and must be collective and inclusive. They need to develop sophisticated, hands-on group design processes to facilitate public participation in the planning and design of multifamily housing and community development beyond the crude, and often unproductive, series of after-the-fact public hearings and environmental impact reports. These are bureaucratic responses too late in the process, when design has been established, the developer's goals set, trust has become impossible, and communities feel they have only the heavy hand of government regulation to protect themselves. All parties must share, from the very beginnings of a design, in that mutual education process between those who hold the long view of environmental and cultural impacts, those who hold the local, and sometimes self-serving view, and those with the shortest view seeking immediate profits from a real-estate deal. Designers can facilitate that process of engagement if they focus their sense of poetry and idealism on designing methods that steer community building as a creative, collective enterprise, at grassroots levels in the earliest stages of a project.

While speed and efficiency are critical to housing production, avoiding the collective design process will only delay production in the long run. The cumulative resistance to change by communities confronting stubborn, self-serving developers will only feed their belief that they are the victims of private profit, often in collusion with local government support. This becomes an immutable inertial force against all growth, self righteously stubborn and ignorant to the values of intelligent growth that may underlie some development proposals. Recognizing that local populations need to be treated as partners in development at the very beginning of design, developers—for profit, non-profit, and public alike—will in the long run improve the climate for achieving higher densities, more compact, mixed-use, and mixed-income communities.

SOCIAL AND ECONOMIC ISSUES

For all its rhetoric about equality, freedom, and justice, the U.S. is fundamentally a deeply divided class society, accentuated by racial and ethnic prejudices. The hope is that, because we continue to extol the virtues of these high principles and keep them at least within our peripheral vision as a nation, we will continue to chip away at the barriers that prevent us from achieving them. Multifamily housing is one more arena within which the struggle to achieve those goals gets a serious workout. Affordable housing, a euphemism for government-assisted housing intended for households whose incomes are too low to pay for market-driven housing, demands special attention by designers.

Stereotypical views about lower-income families and fears by homeowners about property values often get disingenuously expressed as fears about increased traffic, impacts on schools, and rising crime in the streets. While there are deep familial and societal problems caused by the steady loss of better-paying manufacturing jobs and their replacement by low-paying service jobs, often those with the better paying jobs of the new economy harbor misperceptions about their less fortunate fellow citizens victimized by these macro-economic shifts.

It may be asking too much for housing design and neighborhood planning to mellow out the resistance harbored by the middle classes toward mixed-income communities. Yet, when exquisitely designed with a reverence for the local natural and cultural ecology, executed with a sense of poetry, multifamily housing design for lower-income households can throw off balance even the most hardened bigots. They then must resort to complaints about traffic and school impacts to hide their more deeply seated feelings about the future residents. But in any community there are those who, if plagued by doubt, are willing at least to listen to new ideas and beliefs if they are presented with honesty, trust, and openness by developers and their design teams. The design process can be structured upon foundations of designers' personable behavior with no hidden agendas of private or government sources, utilizing transparent participatory design tools.

Separation by economic class, exacerbated by race and ethnicity, will not dissipate quickly. But as long as economically disadvantaged households are short-changed by poor design and planning fueled by under-investment, their communities will be shunned. However, sometimes help from the design community can do more harm than good. Too often the design professions believe that lower-income communities need to be served with the same types of housing as middle-income communities to convey a sense of justice. This is where the social and economic divide can have unforeseen negative consequences. For example, in reaction to the industrialization of the early-20th century, the middle classes came to shape their communities as bucolic retreats from places of work, embracing zoning as a tool to create solely residential neighborhoods cleansed of the many trades and services provided by the under-classes. Years later, middle-class reformists wanting to provide equality of design sought to improve public housing through HUD's HOPE VI program so its neighborhoods and appearances would look more like theirs. But codes and regulations, whether post-World War II or recent traditional neighborhood developments, have systematically made life more difficult for those who need to use their homes as income-producing workshops, stores, or headquarters for other forms of entrepreneurial activity that do not fit the tidy model of domestic retreat.

Those households not benefiting from today's economy face similar survival necessities as their forebears did as colonists, pioneers, or immigrants. With no markets available, colonists and pioneers alike had to design and build new communities whole cloth, using their homes as homesteads, with no bureaucracies monitoring and regulating their every action. Immigrants at the turn of the 20th century often faced similar conditions, closed out of the local economy by language and discrimination. They erected flourishing local economies using their domiciles to build family-based businesses. Today's underclasses face insurmountable regulatory obstacles not experienced by those in the past because they did not exist then. Those obstacles are built into zoning and building codes, insurance policies, lending practices, and property management attitudes that, while ostensibly protecting the health and safety of everyone, too often stifle the entrepreneurial urges of struggling families in the lower economic quartile. Such families often must simply break the law and hope that authorities do not notice or look the other way as they press portions of their homes into uses disallowed by local zoning ordinances or building codes.

A fresh and more creative look needs to be taken at what the definition of home and mixed-use ought to be, of course with an eye towards health and safety issues. But given today's stringent fire codes, many uses presently excluded by zoning from residential neighborhoods could be reinstated. Alley-served neighborhoods offer opportunities for messy private backsides with manicured public front sides. If special fire separations were introduced between front and back portions of alley-served housing, perhaps the back half of a home could entertain such semi-industrial uses as auto repair, appliance repair, sheet-metal assembly, cabinet making, tee-shirt silkscreening, computer assembly, clothing manufacturing, even small restaurants with home cooking by invitation/reservation only.

TECHNOLOGICAL ISSUES

Every generation of architects dreams of that technological silver bullet that will lower the cost of housing, like a medical breakthrough overcoming a centuries-old disease. But this technological mindset always ignores the highly volatile "soft" costs of housing. Some of the soft costs—such as the cost of land, the interest on construction loans or permanent financing, and the profit margins of developers—are all vulnerable to market conditions and can jump up unexpectedly, neutralizing and even reversing any cost reductions resulting even from major technological breakthroughs. The hard costs of construction (labor and materials) constitute about 60 to 70 percent of the production costs of housing, and depending on developers' profit margins and market conditions, total production costs may represent only 50 percent of final sales prices. Assume that a major new construction method—some combination of the execution process and material improvements—could lower production costs by as much as 10 percent. But this may represent only a five percent reduction in sales prices, and just a half-percent jump in the mortgage interest rate could wipe out the savings.

Does this mean architects are wasting their time in seeking technological improvements in production that shorten construction time and material costs? Not necessarily, since non-profit corporations do pass on the savings from technological breakthroughs and this can benefit their production of affordable housing. But single-family infill homes produced by non-profits for first-time buyers can more easily benefit from innovative systems than multifamily.

CONCLUSION

So what should be the main focus of architects' talents? As noted earlier, designing and conducting public participation in the design process to help change both public opinion and that of client-developers is essential to bring about the cultural shifts needed for some very important design innovations. These innovations include smaller units, higher densities, more compact communities with more realistic parking and road standards, mixed-use and mixed-income communities designed to easily accept public transit, energy-efficient strategies that utilize greener materials and systems. Some of these will contribute to lowering first-time costs but some may even raise first-time costs. What is ultimately most important, if all are employed, is that they will lower the long-term costs not just to us as a society but also to the rest of humanity who must, and will, continue to share this planet along with us.

It is that special skill of the architect to bring a compelling sense of poetry to these innovations such that the most hardened skeptics, entrenched in today's self-centered values, might at least turn their heads and admit, "Well, that really isn't half bad after all." That may not be overwhelming praise, but at least that would be a beginning, and in today's world of entrenched ideologies, that would amount to a combined cultural, social, economic, and technological breakthrough.

Michael Pyatok, FAIA
Pyatok Architects

Featured Projects

Bay Bridge

Oakland, California
Pyatok Architects

Housing

Prevented from locating this rental apartment project for low-income singles with AIDS in a residential neighborhood, the developer chose a site that fronts an exit ramp from an elevated eight-lane highway located directly to the south. The site is bound on the west by a barbecue restaurant and a retail street, and on the north and east by single-family homes.

The design goals for Bay Bridge Housing were that it should feel as though it belongs to its location; that it protect the residents from the noise of the highway, exit ramp, and retail street; that it provide respite, inspiration, and uplift to the residents; and that it offer opportunities for individuals to territorialize space while encouraging their resistance to isolation through thoughtful design of such elements as common space and circulation routes.

Instead of relating to the nearby single-family houses the building reflects the adjacent retail uses, filling out the site and matching the height of the restaurant. Four required parking stalls are placed behind two garage doors yet are open to the sky as two quiet pedestrian courts, taking advantage of the fact that the residents do not anticipate owning automobiles. The building shields the units and courtyards from surrounding noise.

Each of the six units faces the main courtyard and has its own front patio and trellis for residents to plant and decorate, encouraging individual expression and informal gatherings. The main court is divided into three smaller and more intimate courts by trellised gateways. As vines cover the trellises and the trees mature, these interconnected courtyards become a quiet and rich garden retreat from the traffic and retail activities of surrounding streets. Residents or visitors must pass through the shared living room near the front of the building when arriving or leaving, encouraging human interaction.

A lattice wall and sunscreens, planted with bougainvillea, forms a "living wall" along with the garden court—a life-affirming symbol promoting optimism, healing, and renewal. The three red birdhouses in front were designed and donated by the architect to encourage further habitation of the living wall.

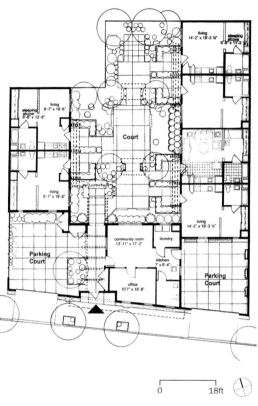

opposite left   Street elevation incorporates living wall
opposite right   Living wall as it faces the sidewalk
right   Architect designed and donated living
        wall birdhouses
above   Site plan

above left   Residents are encouraged to raise gardens
above right   Detail of latticework over walkways
opposite top   Interior courtyard offers respite from neighborhood
opposite bottom   Courtyard structures frame garden areas
photography   Pyatok Architects

Miro Place

Changing demographics in Dallas, especially in inner-city neighborhoods, was in large part a driver of this Miro Place project. A large portion of the area just north of downtown (now known as the Uptown Area) was populated with 1950s and '60s garden apartment complexes, which are no longer economically viable and cannot attract the type of buyers wanting to move into the area.

Miro Place began as a vacant 4.5-acre parcel that was previously the site of an apartment project demolished several years earlier. The owners had completed several apartment renovations in the same neighborhood and saw a need for a product for diverse buyer segments including first time buyers that had been paying high rents in the area, affluent Generation X and Y house hunters, and empty-nesters looking to downsize.

With updated zoning, the site now allowed for a three-story development with closer street setbacks and more favorable variances for landscaping, parking, and common areas. A primary goal became to create a more pedestrian-friendly walking environment by locating all front doors on the street and most garages off alleys to diminish the importance of the car—a fairly new idea in Dallas, where most garages still face directly onto the street. Exterior materials are gray brick, white stucco, and aluminum storefront sash.

These 42 townhome units, ranging from 2,200 to 3,700 square feet, are organized on three levels. The entry/street level consists of a two-car garage and guest suite. The second level houses living, dining, kitchen, and the master bedroom/suite. To accommodate today's informal lifestyle, interior walls in the living and dining room were eliminated, opening the primary living area to a double height volume with a large double height glass wall open to the street, yet raised one level above. This creates a feeling of living in a more cosmopolitan space with an increased sense of security. Situated on the third level is a bedroom/study suite, and in other units a small roof deck.

right   Space hovers over garage entry
opposite top   Fireplace expressed on exterior
opposite bottom   Collection of units has a street presence

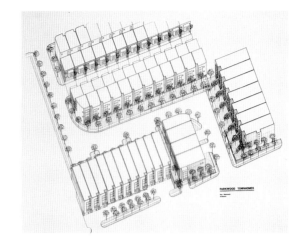

opposite top Units' entries are expressed in stairs
opposite bottom left Vigorous geometries distinguish exterior
opposite bottom right Units as they face south
right Plan of housing
below Stairs to second level of living spaces

top Finely detailed interior
above left Interiors are spacious and light
above right View of living areas from second floor
opposite left Steel beam crosses overhead
opposite right Various plan layouts
photography James F. Wilson

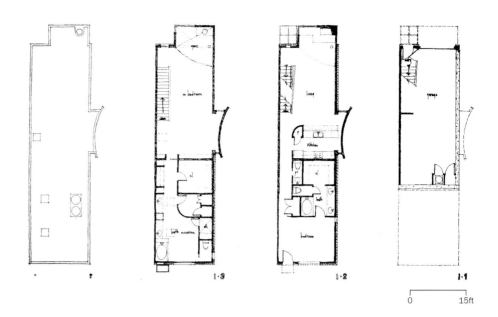

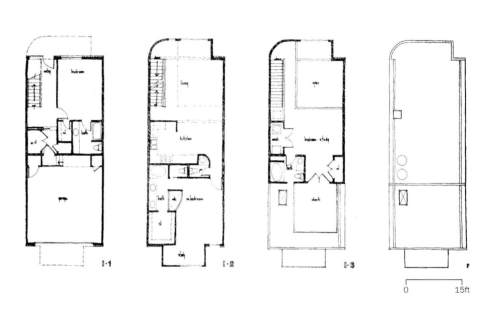

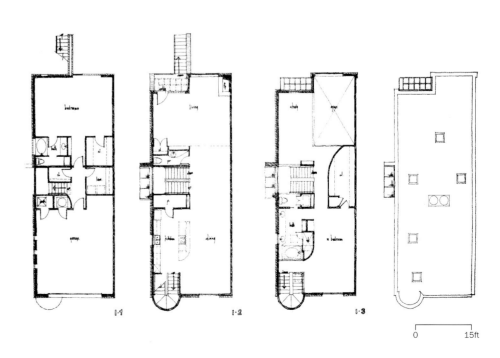

District
Lofts

Toronto, Ontario
architects Alliance

The District Lofts are located on the site of a former parking lot. The design solution involves the development of a somewhat unusual building typology, consisting of retail space at grade, surmounted by two stories of public parking, and 11 floors of residential space above the parking levels. In addition, the building is split into two towers between floors six and 14, with a landscaped central courtyard.

Elevating the residential floors of the building increases the amount of natural light and provides significant views north to the city and south to Lake Ontario. Dividing the building into two towers has also enabled the creation of two-story "through units" serviced by "skip stop" corridors located every other floor. In addition to increasing the saleable area of each floor, the availability of these units significantly increases the amenity level of the building as a whole, and provides excellent circulation of fresh air and daylight.

The amenity level of the building has been raised further through a significant technical innovation. The use of a custom-built underslung elevator system has enabled the architect to move to the basement all the elevator machinery that would be typically located on the penthouse level. In addition, all of the building's mechanical equipment has been located in the basement, enabling the architect to create penthouse residential units with rooftop terraces.

Building materials reflect the context of the surrounding industrial architecture, while communicating the amenity-rich nature of this development. Floors two through five are clad in floating brick panels that echo the traditional masonry of neighboring buildings. Floors six through 14 occupy two graceful towers of sandblasted pre-cast concrete, glass and steel, which convey the character of the District Lofts, while integrating the building into the neighborhood despite its height.

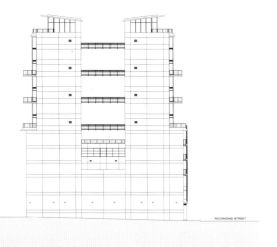

RICHMOND STREET

top left	West elevation
left	Viewed from the east, south elevation opens to sun
opposite top	Detail of south elevation with variety of fenestration
opposite bottom left	West elevation is closed to view of low-rise
opposite bottom right	Building as it faces Richmond Street

below   Units are open and light with floor-to-ceiling windows
opposite top left   Eighth floor plan
opposite middle left   Fourth floor plan
opposite bottom left   First floor plan
opposite right   View of building from Richmond Street
photography   Ben Rahn/Design Archive

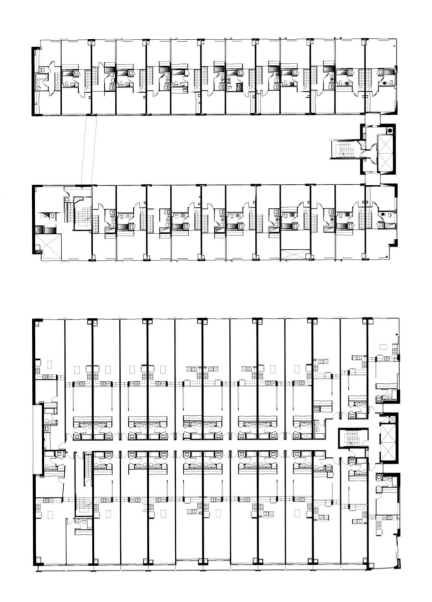

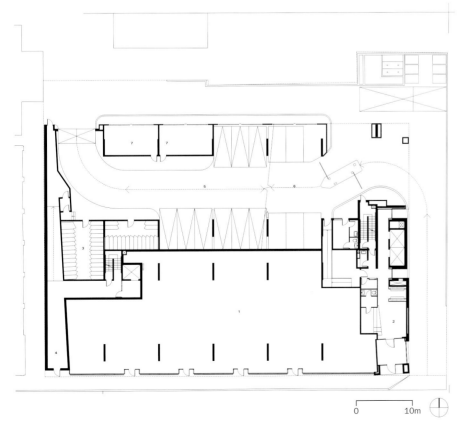

Atherton

Hayward, California
Seidel/Holzman Architecture

Place

The city of Hayward, California is redeveloping its downtown and is particularly interested in locating higher density housing in the blocks surrounding its multi-modal transit station. The BART Station offers convenient transportation throughout the Bay Area, including downtown San Francisco, approximately 40 minutes away.

Following a plan entitled "Recentering" adopted by the city, Atherton Place is the first infill residential development in the area. The almost three-acre site was required to have a minimum of 83 housing units to capitalize on its direct adjacency to the BART station. To accomplish this 30-unit-per-acre density with townhouses, narrow 16-foot-wide units were designed.

Each townhouse has its own stoop entry, with the front door facing either the street or the inner courtyard. The other side of the dwelling faces the inner lane, which accommodates both the garage doors and a rear entry into the townhouse. Since only one garage space per unit was required due to transit adjacency, each unit has only one eight-foot-wide garage door, which considerably improves the architectural character of the inner lane. Many units incorporate a second covered parking space in the tandem fashion, which was considered to be desirable from a marketing standpoint even though it was not required.

The compact 1,250-square-foot to 1,500-square-foot townhouses are planned to maximize openness and light. Each townhouse has a small walled patio, and the central courtyard contains a pool and other community amenities. A massing of paired townhouses was developed to create the residential scale of the street frontages. Various details and colors were utilized to highlight the individuality of these pairs along the block. Fenestration, ornamental metal, bay windows, trellises, and awnings are some of the details that vary within an overall unified architectural character.

A number of surrounding blocks are now being developed with dense housing, giving rise to a contemporary urban neighborhood with strong pedestrian character and pleasing streetscapes. Within easy walking distance of downtown amenities and transit, the neighborhood is offering residents an alternative to the suburban single-family home historically prevalent in the area.

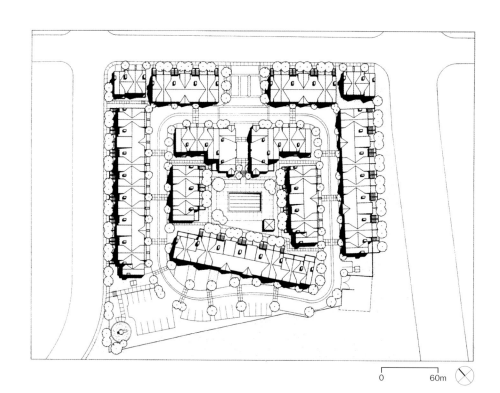

0   60m

opposite top   Strong colors distinguish façades
opposite bottom   Site plan
top   Street elevation
above   Pulling back from sidewalk offers buffer space
right   Protective walls provide private outdoors space

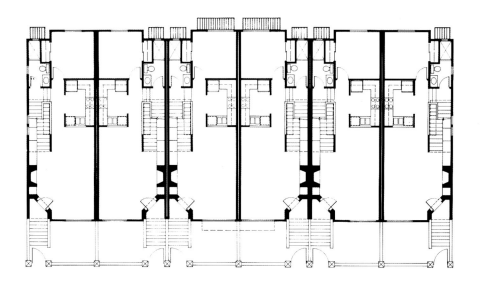

opposite top left   Views are encouraged between living spaces
opposite top right   Light fills interiors from ample fenestration
opposite bottom   Typical row units
below left   Interiors offer uninterrupted living areas
below right   Staircase is naturally illuminated from above
bottom   Typical end units
photography   Gerald Ratto

Block X

Chicago, Illinois
Pappageorge/Haymes Architects

The light industrial buildings and lofts prevalent in the area of this development are respected in the design of this residential complex with its position on the edge of the sidewalk and use of red brick, masonry, and glass, which recall the architectural flavor of the neighborhood. Block X (named after the configuration of an early site plan) answers the need for upscale multifamily housing in this urban precinct.

Enter this gated community, however, and the environment is transformed. Five buildings fill the perimeter of the 1.77-acre site, leaving a one-third acre park on the interior as an oasis in the city. The park is lushly landscaped, with unit terraces, decks, and porches overlooking the greenery. Color plays against the terra cotta brick, metal panels, painted steel, and blue hand railings. The façades are active with fenestration changes, terraces, and balconies, and the extensive landscaping is visually lively. Simple materials, such as brick and cinderblock, lend an honest, straightforward appearance to the entire project.

A driving force in the design is unseen. Parking for 112 cars is located beneath the buildings and garden, which allows more space to be devoted above-ground to amenities. The buildings encompass 100 units in two elevator buildings at the main entrance, two walk-up buildings on the sides, and 12 townhomes with four penthouses on the end. Units range in size from 750 to 2,340 square feet. A blue steel canopy, suspended from garage ventilation shaft towers, distinguishes the main entrance to Block X.

above left   Variety of materials distinguish exteriors
opposite top   Street side expresses warehouse context
opposite bottom   Frames define balconies on second floor

opposite top left   Urban scale is captured in tower forms
opposite top middle   Detail of circulation tower façade
opposite top right   Pathways lend courtyard pedestrian scale
opposite bottom   Pathways are found throughout public spaces
above   Low scale of buildings softens courtyard

below left   Slight curve in façades follow contour of courtyard
below right   Green courtyard is the project's major amenity
opposite top   Exhaust ducts support canopy structure
opposite bottom   Entry is distinguished with a canopy
photography   Pappageorge/Haymes

Santa Monica

Santa Monica, California
David Forbes Hibbert, AIA

Art Colony

This project is designed to provide combined housing and work space for individuals and small businesses within the creative design and art community of Santa Monica. The project is home to several annual open studio events. The tenants range from a core of traditional artists to multi-media artists and studio set designers.

Arranged around a courtyard, the housing is connected by a series of walkways to encourage community and collaboration amongst the tenants. The arrangement of the lofts lends itself to open studio events with the large central court functioning as a gathering point while the walkways provide for the smaller gatherings around the work of particular tenants.

In addition to the arrangement of units relative to shared spaces, the individual units are provided with public and private faces, through primary or street access and rear door service access. Each unit is also open to either a private deck or small landscaped area. For the two-story lofts this private area is large enough for exterior art projects; electricity is provided for welding and other industrial art processes. On the interior, large, minimally finished warehouse-like shells are free for embellishment as suits the type of art/design work of the particular tenant.

This live/work project has provided a test case for the City of Santa Monica public approval process. The concept of live/work, while heavily encouraged by the City of Santa Monica Planning Commission, was not addressed in the building design requirements of local and state codes. The project team worked with building department officials to mold non-applicable and conflicting code requirements into interpretations and modifications of the code appropriate for the maintenance of the functional and aesthetic integrity of a live/work loft project. In particular, the design satisfies the strict requirements for fire and life safety while maintaining large open lofts with exposed structures, favored by artists for the good light quality and large bare work areas. The community is served by shared underground parking, a freight elevator, and a loading dock sized for large product delivery.

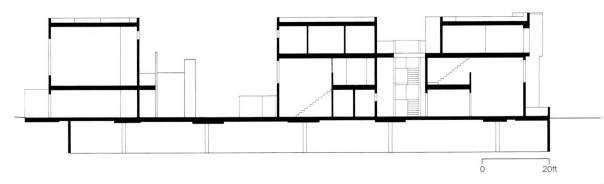

opposite   Units are domestic in scale
top   Section
above   Building offers glimpses into site
left   Geometry of complex is expressive

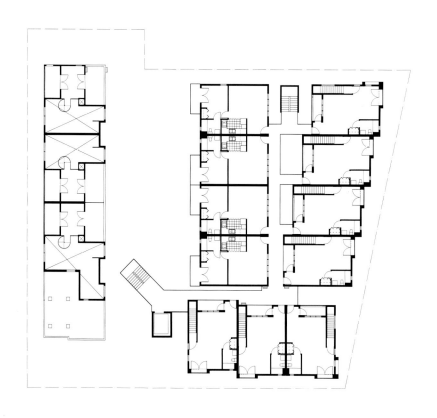

0   25ft

top   Third floor plan
above   First floor plan
opposite   Quiet courtyard affords units privacy
photography   Benny Chan

above left   Interiors are simple but elegantly detailed
photography   Katherine Jones
above right   Exposed structure as seen from below
below left   Light fills space from above
below right   View of living area from second floor
photography   Charles Swanson
opposite   Roof structure lends character to space
photography   Benny Chan

Ellen Wilson Place

Washington, D.C.
Weinstein Associates Architects

This project is a model, new mixed-income community, both economically and racially. A determined, diverse group of community and business leaders, working with the architect and developers from concept to completion, was responsible for the redevelopment of an abandoned 134-unit public housing project into a seamless extension of the surrounding community's character, income, and racial mix. Development costs were fully funded by a HUD HOPE VI grant and the project requires no ongoing public subsidy.

The 5.3-acre site is surrounded by the Victorian era Capitol Hill Historic District on three sides and is bordered on the fourth by an elevated highway. Designed to leave no discernible edge between itself and the surrounding community, the new housing and streets are modeled on Capitol Hill's historic development pattern: rarely were blocks developed uniformly with one typical building type lining both sides of the street. Far more prevalent are blocks where only three or four buildings in a row are the same type.

Ellen Wilson Place is tightly developed with street trees sharing parallel parking areas and relatively shallow house lots. A new mews building type provides private side yards in lieu of rear yards and side front entry to allow a sense of private separation from the narrow public sidewalk. The new housing provides architectural definition to both the new and existing streets. The 36 different façade designs and five different building types are deployed to evoke the sporadic and staccato rhythms of Capitol Hill housing. Additional variety is introduced through the use of 22 different bricks, 17 mortar colors, eight window colors for the 30 window sizes, and 15 ornamental stair-railing designs.

Through the use of computer-driven cutting (laser, plasma-jet, etc.), ornamental architectural elements such as wood cornice brackets and metal stair risers have been achieved within the project budget. The use of special shaped bricks affords an economical means to introduce patterning into façades and articulation of window openings. Careful study of proportions brings each façade affordably into the Capitol Hill spirit.

opposite   Brick sidewalks lend to variety of textures and scale
right   Variety allows for multiple scales along the street
below   Rusticated stone is used on typical façade

opposite   Color lends strong personality to townhouse units
above   Color, details, and texture animate façades
below   Street elevation

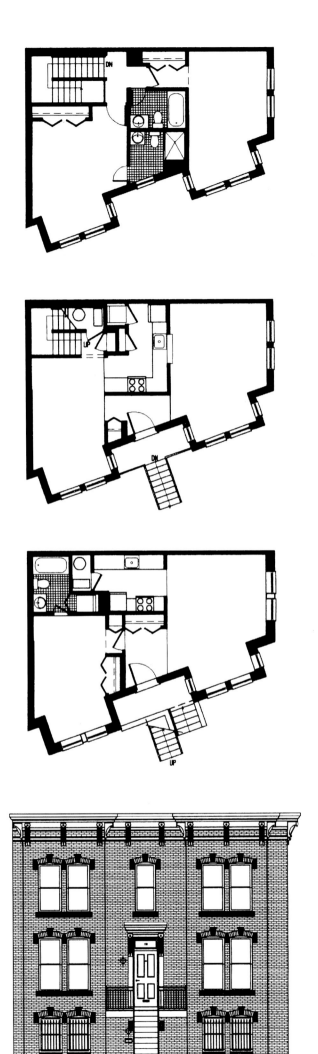

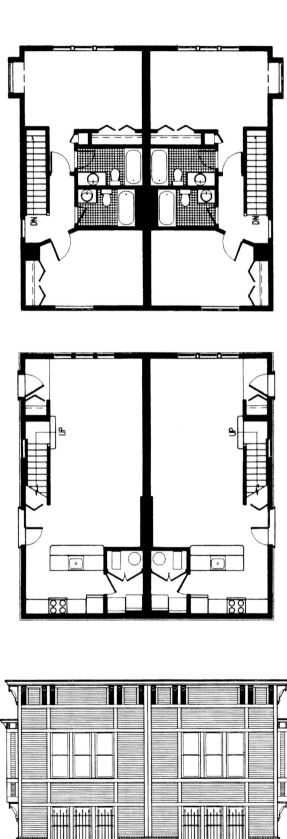

opposite left   Building type 5, floor plans and elevation
opposite right   Building type 4, floor plans and elevation
below   Row houses are a common building type in neighborhood
photography   Hoachlander Davis Photography

Silvercrest

Puyallup, Washington
Pyatok Architects

Senior Housing

Located on a busy neighborhood street a few blocks from a major retail district, Silvercrest is conceived as a residential "lodge." While being a larger building called home by 41 senior singles or couples, it needed to fit on a street lined with single-family homes. Being subsidized by the federal government for very low-income seniors, the building also needed to calm the fears of local residents with a comfortable and familiar vocabulary. A colorful and cheerful country inn was chosen as the image both for the sake of the senior residents and the neighbors. This region has a large number of older Scandinavian immigrants, and the colors recall Scandinavian farm buildings.

The three-story building is L-shaped to create an east- and south-facing back court, private from the street, leaving room for a wetlands on the site fed by a creek along its south edge. Placing the north wing perpendicular to the street conceals the building's size from public view. The main body of the building facing the street drops to two stories near the creek to soften its impact.

The laundry room and an adjacent lounge are located just above the front entry and open onto a deck above the front porch. The laundry lounge, an important social place, is designed to meet another need by seniors: to watch the street and the comings and goings in their shared home. The main multipurpose room opens onto the rear patio. A cozy fireplace nook is placed just off the crossroads of first floor traffic to induce casual social encounters. Its open yet retreating quality allows seniors to watch the ebb and flow of life in their home yet feel they are in an intimate, safe place.

Each unit has a bay window providing light and views from several directions and to expand the sense of space. Each kitchen has an interior corner window facing the corridor to allow residents to monitor their entry porches and corridor as well as to increase social exchanges.

opposite left   Window bays allow views throughout the complex
opposite right   Courtyard offers a protected place
left   Front of building appears like a large home
below   Site plan

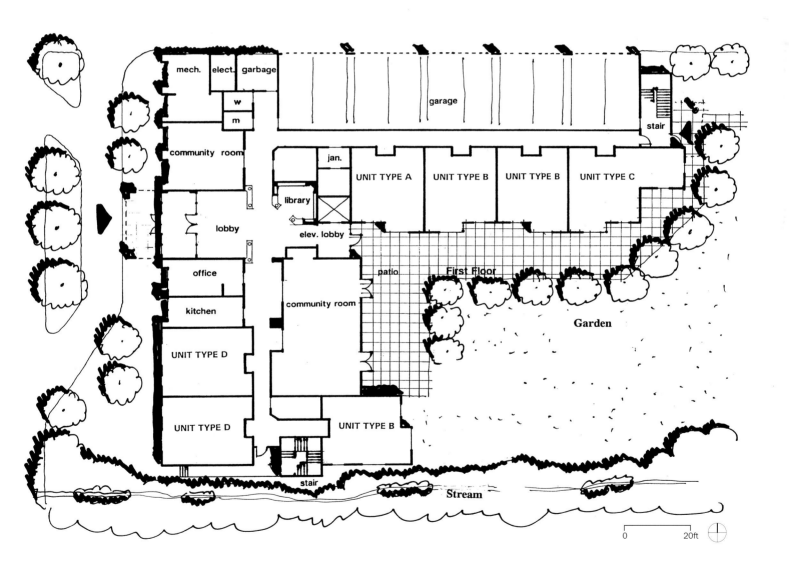

mech.   elect. garbage

w

m

garage

community room

stair

jan.

library

UNIT TYPE A   UNIT TYPE B   UNIT TYPE B   UNIT TYPE C

lobby

elev. lobby

office

patio

First Floor

kitchen

community room

Garden

UNIT TYPE D

UNIT TYPE D

UNIT TYPE B

stair

Stream

0   20ft

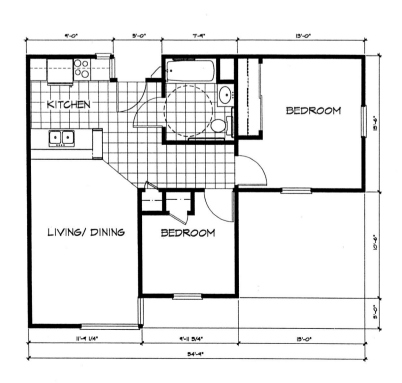

opposite top   Bright colors suggest Scandinavian design roots
opposite bottom left   Unit D, floor plan
opposite bottom right   Unit C, floor plan
below left   Scale and colors fit well in wooded setting
below middle   Wood siding contributes to building's domestic appearance
below left   Materials contribute to building sensitive scale
bottom left   Unit A/B, floor plan
bottom right   Unit E, floor plan
photography   Pyatok Architects

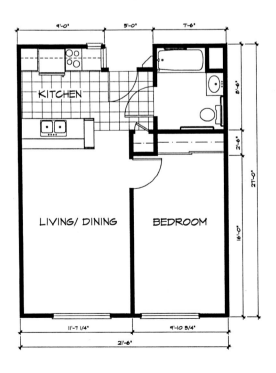

Pierce

Houston, Texas
RTKL

Elevated

An inspired loft building in Houston makes the most of its urban location. Rather than shrink from an elevated expressway two blocks away, Pierce Elevated rises above it. By placing 129 loft residential units on top of three levels of above-grade parking, most of the double-height units in the building have unobstructed views through 19-foot-tall windows to downtown, just four blocks away. This also raises the living space above the noise and dust of the highway, and gives residents commanding views of the city.

Realizing that visibility is a two-way street, Pierce Elevated has a distinctive architectural roof form and sculptural canopy over the resident roof terrace. This eye-catching element acts as a billboard, appealing to the thousands of motorists who pass it each day. The building's materials include brick, concrete, glass, and steel, giving it a sleek appearance. The finely-detailed glass bays emerge from its concrete structural frame.

To maintain neighborhood scale and to make the project economically viable, a 56-unit, four-story wood frame building compliments the 15-story tower, while also defining a retail motor court for patron, visitor, and guest parking. This gives Pierce Elevated a variety of living scales, with a counterpoint between high-rise and low-rise accommodations.

Residents also enjoy a rooftop terrace over the parking structure that features a linear fountain and a fireplace that encourages community gatherings. Some units have individual secured garages and all exhibit distinctive two-level floor plans, floor-to-ceiling glass, and an attitude that is anything but pedestrian.

opposite left   Site plan
opposite right   Building's glass personality is revealed at night
top   Building's presence on the skyline
above   Parking is found in first few floors

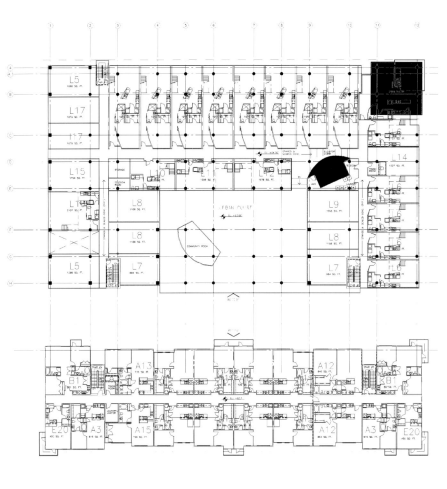

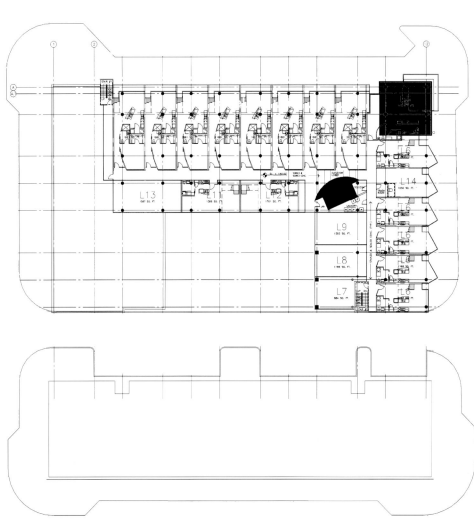

Russellville
Commons

Portland, Oregon
MCM Architects

Russellville Commons revives an abandoned, 10.5-acre lot adjacent to Portland's MAX Light Rail line. The site (formerly occupied by a school) is near downtown Portland in an area of older, modest single-family homes and mixed commercial uses. Zoned for retail/commercial, the site was initially studied for potential strip retail development. However, the project's developer, The Rembold Companies, elected to pursue a more enlightened program better suited to the needs of the neighborhood. The program for Phase One consists of 283 one-, two-, and three-bedroom apartments in a series of three-story buildings.

The site design restores the adjacent street grid that had been interrupted by the school, while avoiding the standard suburban apartment building layout of a street fronted by parking with living units beyond. Portland's 200 by 200-foot grid creates an intimate, pedestrian streetscape reinforced by placing all of the buildings immediately adjacent to the street and locating parking in the rear at the center of each block. Ground- and second-level porches, together with low walls to define private, outdoor space, further reinforce the pedestrian quality while maintaining an appropriate balance of public and private space. A landscaped "Park Block" in the middle of the development provides additional open space and a pedestrian spine connecting to the rail line to the north.

The buildings are arranged with one-bedroom flats on the first floor and two- and three-bedroom townhouses above. All the front doors face the street. Entry to the one-bedroom flats is through a patio while the townhouses have an adjacent street-level front door that leads to a private stair. The form of the building allows the third floor to be nestled under the sloped roof, thereby reducing the overall height of the buildings and providing an archetypal house form, familiar and comfortable within the neighborhood. Color has been used liberally to define the buildings on each block and to further enhance their identity. The colors have been chosen for their liveliness and their ability to convey a rich warm palette even during Portland's gray, rainy winters.

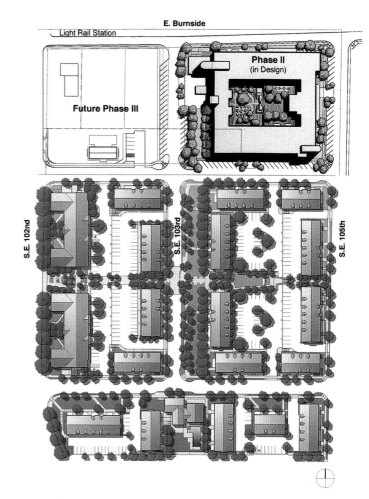

opposite left   Landscaping helps soften building edge
opposite right   Site plan
right top   Gable roofs establish a domestic scale
right bottom   View across complex of buildings
below   Unit fronts are shaded with trellis and balconies

top left	Detail of trellis structure
top right	Balcony/porch elements contribute privacy
above left	Ample open space between unit blocks
above right	Exterior is articulated with wood members
opposite top	Typical building section
opposite bottom left	Detail of balcony/porch structures
opposite bottom right	Bright colors distinguish exterior

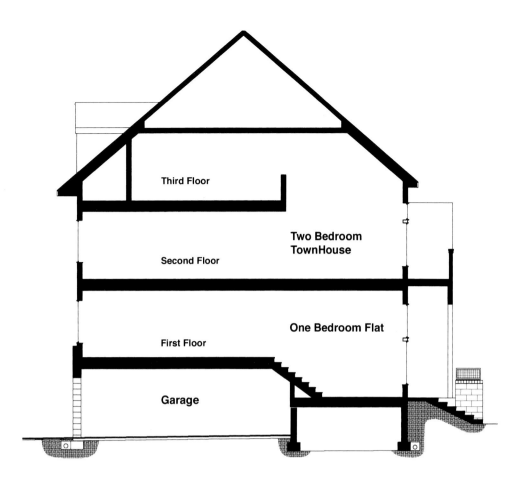

Third Floor

Second Floor

First Floor

Garage

Two Bedroom
TownHouse

One Bedroom Flat

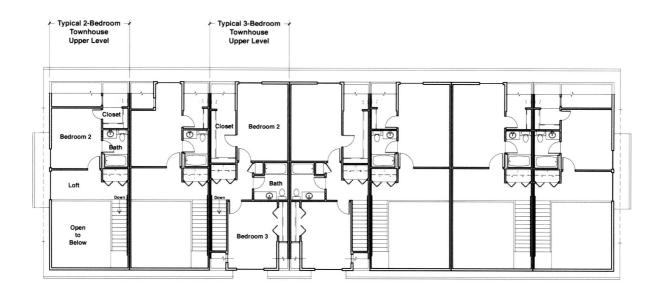

Typical 2-Bedroom Townhouse Upper Level

Typical 3-Bedroom Townhouse Upper Level

Closet

Bedroom 2

Bath

Loft

Open to Below

Down

Closet

Bedroom 2

Bath

Bedroom 3

Down

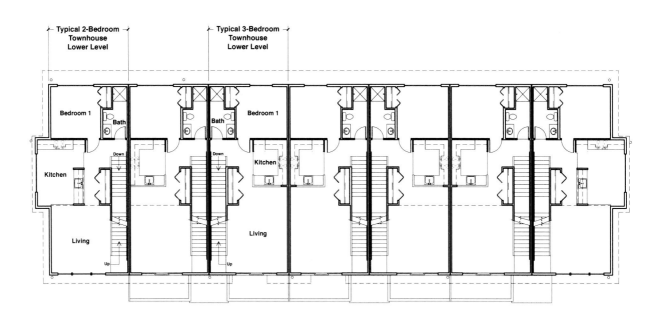

Typical 2-Bedroom Townhouse Lower Level

Typical 3-Bedroom Townhouse Lower Level

Bedroom 1

Bath

Kitchen

Living

Down

Up

Bedroom 1

Bath

Kitchen

Living

Down

Up

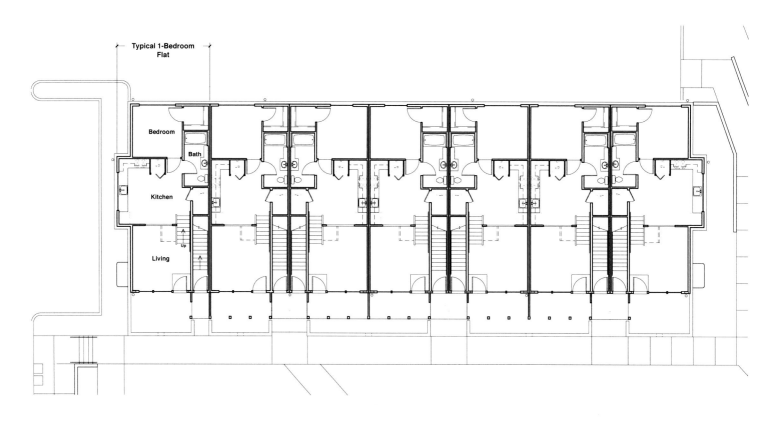

Typical 1-Bedroom Flat

Bedroom

Bath

Kitchen

Living

Up

Summit Residence
Halls and Court

Trinity College, Hartford, Connecticut
William Rawn Associates, Architects

This residence complex and court consists of 173 beds in apartment-style layouts, in four- and six-story buildings on the top of a plinth or plateau—a powerful example of fitting moderately large residential buildings into a tight site. The first set of buildings constructed under a new master plan that was initiated by the college's president, the complex follows a strategy of filling in missing teeth and strengthening the series of four quadrangles from south to north. This residential project sets a standard of materials and organization that will be followed by the next three buildings that will follow.

The building seeks to be decidedly sculptural, which can be read as a raised accent, in order to complete the quad. The complex is joined to the quad by a 12-foot-wide ramp with occasional steps, which acts more like a medieval ramp entering an Italian hill town. It speaks of entry to the new raised court, yet its width and gentle slope create an almost seamless connection to the larger quad below.

The complex employs several architectural strategies. A long "bar" building acts as an anchor to the project and includes a portal that refers to the existing traditional buildings in a Modernist way. The buildings on the interior of the court create a more sculptural form in plan, and feature a six-story tower as a centerpiece. This tower announces the arrival of the college from the south and refers to the college's chapel tower—an iconic image farther to the north. The tower's form is non-historic, forming a head to a linear building without resorting to traditional gable or pyramid tower forms. It also signals the importance of the residence hall complex to the campus.

opposite left   Summit south wing as it backs onto woods
opposite right   Summit tower's tutorial spaces open to court
right   Site plan
below   Summit tower as it surveys the court

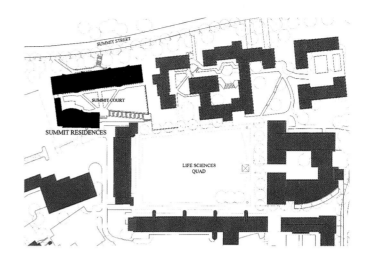

opposite   Approach to Summit tower and court from north
below   Unit suite floor plan
bottom   Ground floor plan

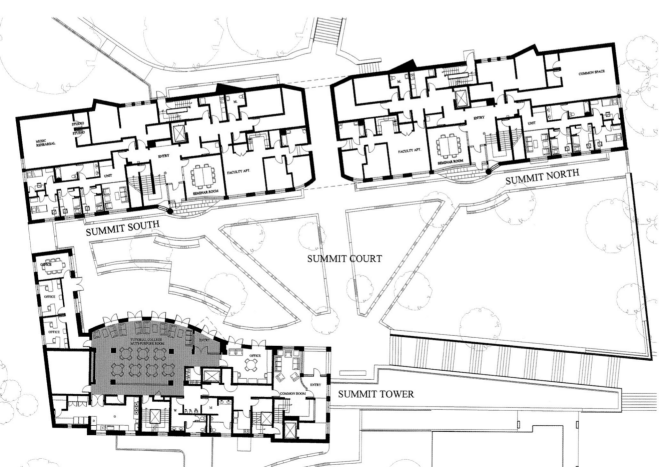

left   Summit tower's tutorial college and multipurpose room
top   Curved overhang helps define entrance
above   Study area in Summit tower
photography   Steve Rosenthal

Cupertino Park Center

Cupertino, California
Seidel/Holzman Architecture

Adherence to single-family residential zoning, combined with the intense job creation of Silicon Valley, has left the community of Cupertino with a significant jobs/housing imbalance. The resultant traffic problems and lack of a sense of community have led the city to revise its policies to promote the development of high-density housing, and to greatly curtail additional office and R&D development.

Cupertino Park is a high-density apartment community located within a commercial/mixed-use master plan conceived in the early 1980s. Facing a community park and flanked by midrise suburban office buildings, the apartments strike an urban note with individual stoop entries and contemporary massing.

Parking is subterranean and is provided in two below-grade levels, creating a podium courtyard to which many of the apartments open. The main courtyard entry opens to the park with a grand stairway ascending from the street. Color variations are employed to emphasize the vertical massing, and create a pedestrian scale to the street frontages.

With 120 apartments on little over 1.5 acres, Cupertino can accomplish 12 to 15 times its historical residential density, and at the same time begin to establish a center to its community. The project creates an active mixed-use environment throughout the day by combining office space, residential units, and a restaurant in a single structure. A public plaza faces DeAnza Boulevard, creating a gateway into Cupertino's central business district, while a more sheltered courtyard to the west is a quiet pedestrian-oriented entry to the site.

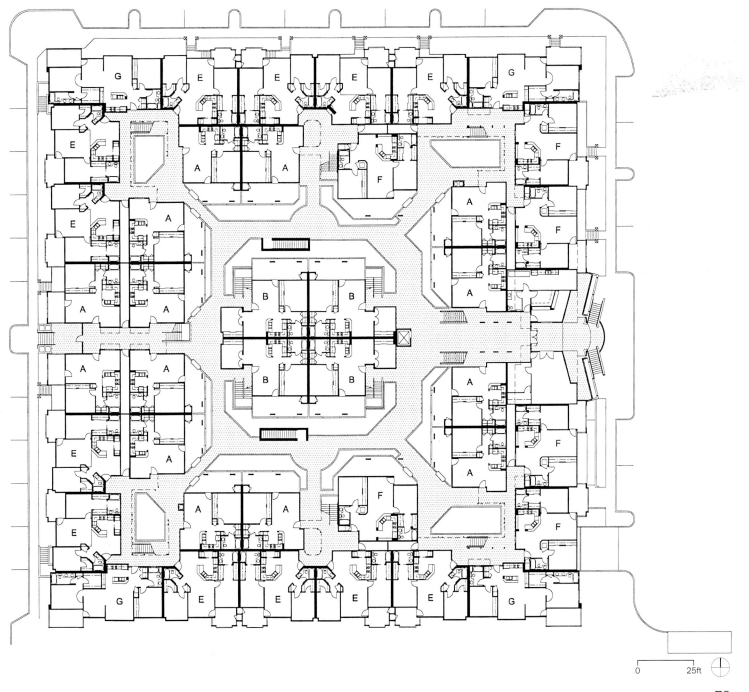

opposite Elevations are highly articulated in geometry
right Welcoming façade on east elevation
below Podium floor plan

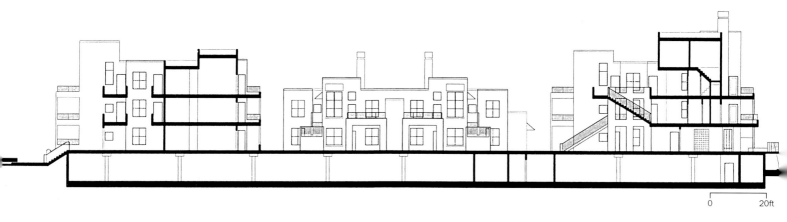

opposite top   West–east site section
opposite bottom   Courtyard paths contribute to domestic scale
top   Kitchens are open and share space with dining
above   Interior spaces are light and flowing
photography   Tom Rider

Old Town
Lofts

Portland, Oregon
Robertson, Merryman, Barnes Architects

Fitting in with the neighborhood was a major goal of the design of this 60-unit project. The context included modest, early-1900 brick buildings. The design also sought to incorporate the lively visual character of Chinatown. The program included units for a variety of family sizes, incomes, and preferences. Because of the dense urban site, views and daylighting were maximized.

Situated in Portland's Old Town/Chinatown neighborhood, the building enjoys views of the new Portland Classical Chinese Garden (Lan Su Yuan), the river and bridges, and the city skyline. It responds to the context with decorative translucent screening at the parking level that recalls "leak" windows in the Chinese Garden and other Chinese motifs including the eighth-floor logia, which mimics traditional Chinatown inset balconies. At the corner, the design recognizes its gateway location at the north end of NW Fourth Street, with Chinatown's lion gates at the south end of Fourth at Burnside. Brick and concrete respond to the character of the older neighborhood warehouses, and windows are maximized in the units but organized so that the building still looks appropriate in its context by using double-hung units.

The internal courtyard and partial single-loaded corridors allow maximum daylighting in the units and views from the corridor. Small, inset "Romeo" balconies provide efficient connections to the exterior and architectural depth and relief on the exterior. The 13 different unit designs range in size from 600 to 1,670 square feet, including penthouse townhouse units.

This project incorporates a number of sustainable design elements. For example, more than 98 percent of demolition waste from the existing buildings was recycled. New cabinets are constructed of wheat straw board, concrete with fly ash is used as both exposed finish and as structural system, and a central energy-efficient water-loop heat-pump system allows trade-offs between different orientations and time-of-day energy needs. In addition, partial overhangs on the south elevations protect some of the largest windows from summer sun, and double-hung windows provide ventilation. The eighth-floor logia and trellis encourage greenery and landscaping for sun shading.

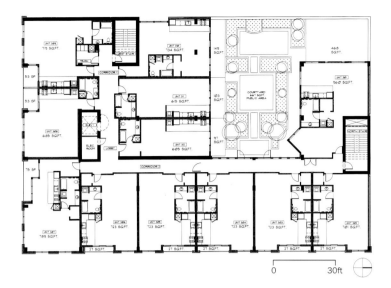

opposite left   At the corner of Fourth and Burnside
opposite right   Brick buildings in area influenced façade design
left   Third floor plan with courtyard
bottom left   Loggia at building's top
bottom right   Building's presence at corner

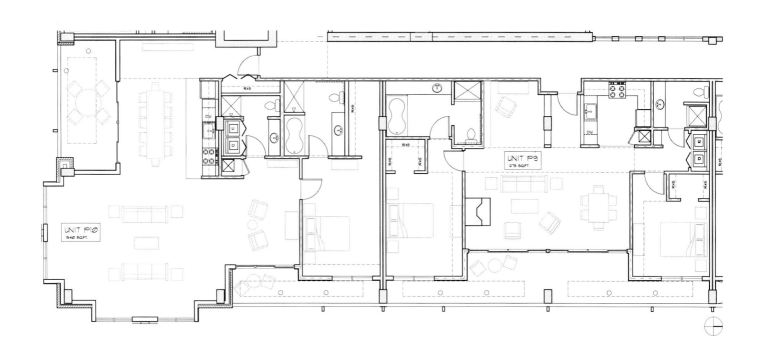

UNIT P10
1540 SQ.FT.

UNIT P9
1275 SQ.FT.

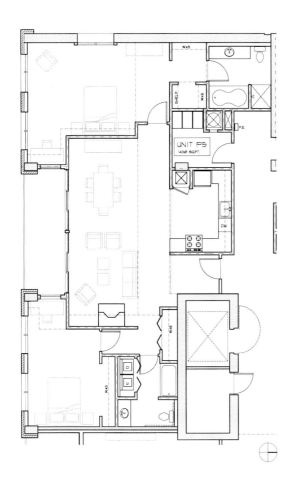

UNIT P8
1430 SQ.FT.

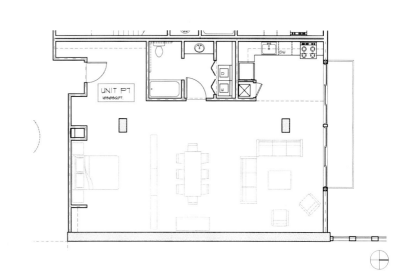

UNIT P7
1050 SQ.FT.

opposite   Penthouse unit, floor plans
below left   Inset windows offer shade
below right   Detail of corner

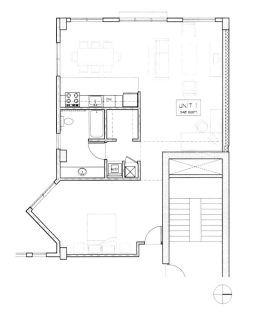

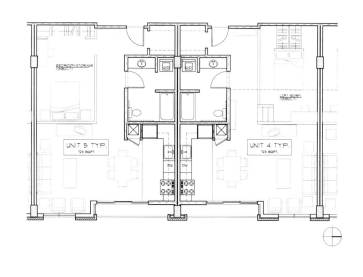

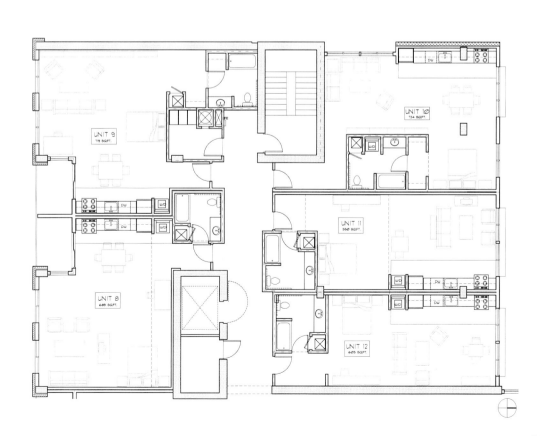

Lakeview
Commons

Chicago, Illinois
Pappageorge/Haymes Architects

Uniquely canted steel bay windows bring variety and distinction to a group of townhouses located on a compact former industrial site at the emerging edge of Chicago's Lincoln Park neighborhood.

Forming a bridge between a recently converted loft building and a development of single-family homes, the site plan efficiently accommodates 30 contemporary townhouses in two rows. The arrangement creates two distinct zones. A public face, with raised front doors looking onto Diversey Avenue, brings the project strong identity and urban presence. An inner row of nine units completes the building's form and bounds a quiet drive, which provides access to garages but also doubles as a courtyard. Each townhouse is given a private front yard, shielded by a brick screen wall. The form of the outer row of homes is broken to allow a glimpse into the inner court and provide pedestrian access to the street.

Subtle tone-on-tone shifts in brick color and vertical separation created by colored downspouts distinguish individual units while maintaining a cohesive appearance. Color also serves to highlight other architectural elements such as canopies, stairs, handrails, and window frames. A sense of drama is added through the use of outward canted steel bays, painted in a soft blue-green. The bays bring a sense of openness to the interior rooms while increasing space, and also provide views up and down the street. Corners are emphasized through orthogonal wrap-around bays. Each townhouse culminates in a large, private roof deck, providing skyline views.

below Large fenestration openings lend bright interiors
opposite top left Project has low walls that define private precincts
opposite top right Alternating bays have sloped glazing
opposite bottom Three-story project defines street edge
photography Pappageorge/Haymes

Bernal
Gateway

San Francisco, California
Pyatok Architects

Bernal Gateway is located on an irregularly shaped sloping parcel in the dense neighborhood fabric of the Mission District. The architect worked closely with neighborhood groups to shape a design that accommodated the new family housing, open play areas, and extensive community facilities while respecting the scale and character of the surrounding neighborhood. The ground floor facing Mission and Cesar Chavez streets houses a childcare center and the "Family School," a neighborhood-based adult education center. At the interior of the site, townhomes face a series of stepped courtyards linked together by a private through-block passage.

This 55-unit affordable family housing development is the result of an extensive participatory design process using building kits and involving about 75 residents of the Bernal Heights neighborhood in five design teams to explore options. The resulting design includes a "street wall" boulevard building that wraps the corner of Mission and Chavez streets, the main crossroads of the neighborhood. The ground floor's neighborhood adult school and childcare center are designed to assist lower income families to become economically self-sufficient and language proficient.

Behind this front building are four courtyards on three levels in the center of the block surrounded by family townhomes stacked above accessible flats. Two of the courts are above the parking garage. This cluster of mid-block "cottages" shapes a small village with play areas secure from the surrounding busy streets. The rear of the property faces Precita Street, a narrow residential thoroughfare. Two of the units are arranged in a duplex to relate to that more intimate public edge.

The adult school, an important neighborhood institution, has its entry at the corner of the street-wall building facing Mission and Chavez. The housing is entered from Mission Street through a two-story open paseo leading to an interior courtyard shared by the childcare center's play yard. The 45-auto garage beneath the two central courtyards is entered from Mission Street. A courtyard behind the duplex on Precita contains an area for the tenants' vegetable garden.

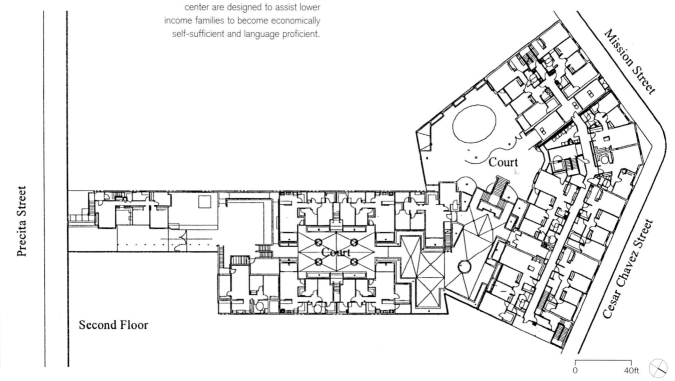

Precita Street

Court

Court

Mission Street

Cesar Chavez Street

Second Floor

0   40ft

opposite Site plan
left Interior of courtyard offers variety of scales
below Color and massing break up façade

top left   Tile distinguishes building's base
top right   Smaller units are found on ends
right   Entry is marked by canopy element
opposite top   Color and fenestration contribute to domestic design
opposite bottom   Architecture is domestically scaled

above　　　　Units as they help define courtyard
below　　　　Units create small piazzas deep in complex
opposite top　　Ground floor plan, Building I
opposite bottom　Second floor plan, Building III
photography　　Pyatok Architects

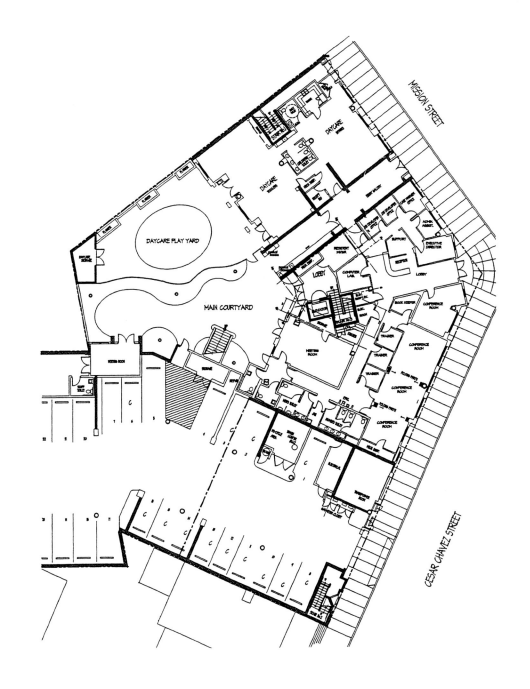

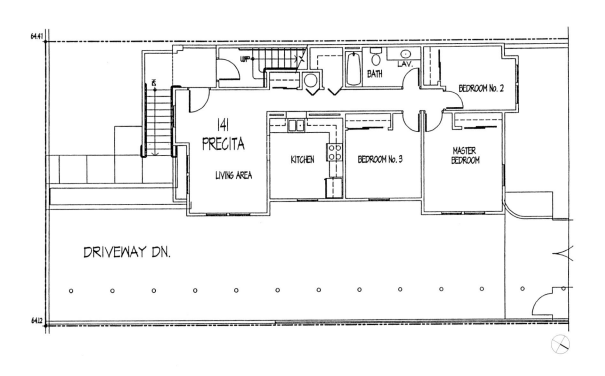

Ballpark

Hoboken, New Jersey
Sergio Guardia Architects

Hoboken is part of the New York City metropolitan area, connected to the city by subway and ferry. The site for this new multifamily building with rental apartments was originally a late 19th-century industrial zone, which is now in the early stages of residential gentrification. Nearby blocks are comprised of industrial buildings and a football field for the local high school team. The site includes two existing industrial buildings, one built in the early 1900s and the other in the 1950s.

The project consists of 64 apartments in three different buildings, two extant, each with their own language and era. The three buildings, forming an L in plan, are connected to each other at every floor. The L-shaped courtyard contains parking for 50 cars.

The new building, connected to the 1950s addition, consists of a five-story structure containing 14 apartments. The ground floor accommodates the lobby and 14 covered parking spaces. The new structure does not mimic the surrounding buildings. On the contrary, it acquires a residential scale and language of its own. The building becomes an abstract approach of the neighborhood's industrial fabric through the use of large fenestration, ground-face concrete block, and stucco panels.

The building is set back and creates balconies and exterior corridors. Volumes are defined, creating a dynamic façade. The apartments are laid out to take advantage of the orientation and views. The units on the top two floors are duplexes in order to maximize the number of units with views of the New York skyline.

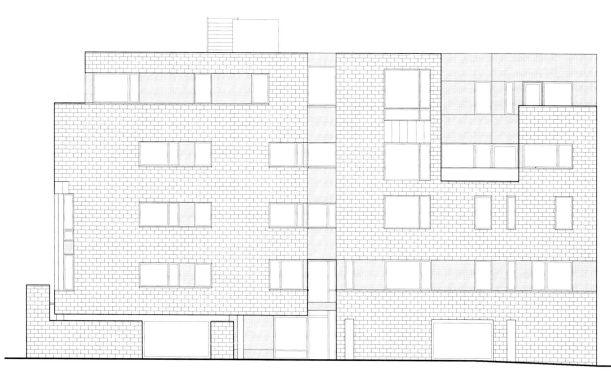

opposite top   New building on left as it connects to existing
opposite bottom   East elevation
right   Exterior is simply detailed
below   Building as it edges next to the ballpark

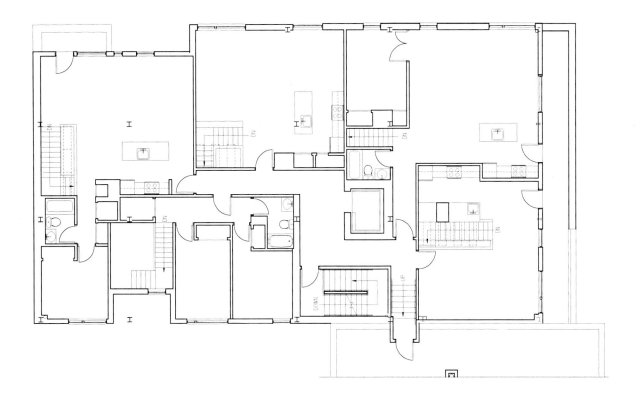

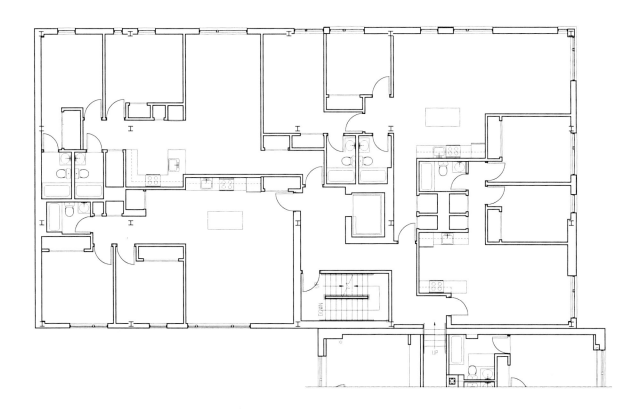

Metro Center-
Citypark

Foster City, California
Seidel/Holzman Architecture

Three components comprise this project: 60 units of affordable senior housing, 40 townhouses, and a town green. Together they complete a mixed-use suburban town center that also includes office and retail uses in immediate proximity. The intention of the design was to weave together formerly disconnected structures and uses in the neighborhood, create a vibrant and active town green for the community, and to produce a diverse mixed income, mixed generation, high density residential neighborhood. The project is a joint development by the Foster City Redevelopment Agency, a nonprofit developer, and a for-profit developer.

The housing brackets two sides of the town square. The multiple clients were persuaded to share the two residential sites, as opposed to each taking a site individually. This permitted the creation of two residential courtyards defined by townhouses on the perimeter and a five-story building for seniors in the center. Miniparks enliven the courtyards, which also accommodate vehicular access. The street and town-square frontages were developed as strong pedestrian frontages with stoop entries, bay windows, and ornamental metal detailing.

Pedestrian connections lead from the residential courtyards to the completely reconfigured town green. Formerly lacking adequate circulation and amenities, the town green now has broad brick-paved promenades connecting the office, retail, and residential uses. Benches, lighting, a clock tower, planting, and small plazas have made the town green a highly successful destination as well as a crossroads for the community.

The senior buildings are designed around an atrium communal space that provides access to the units. The use of tandem parking for the townhouses allows higher density but with fewer garage entrances. A unique, one-sided townhouse was designed to back up to retail loading docks adjacent to the residential site.

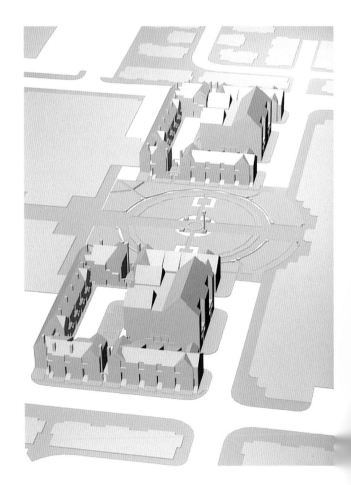

opposite left   Roofs, chimney, doorways help articulate façades
opposite right   Overall perspective view
left   Courtyard between projects is marked with clock tower
below   Green space provides appropriate foreground

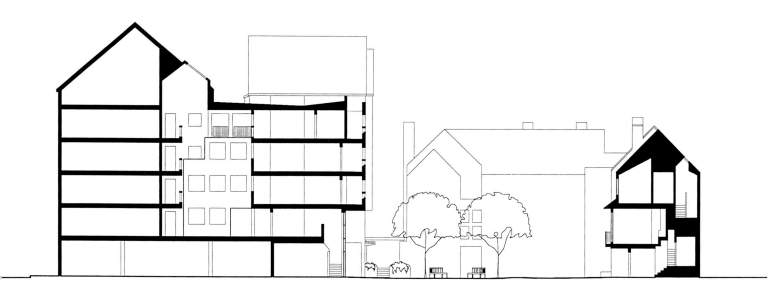

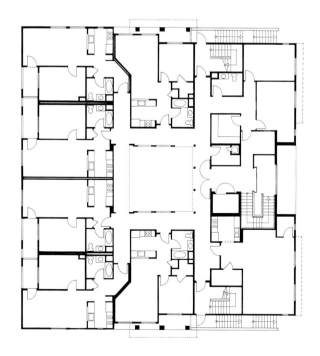

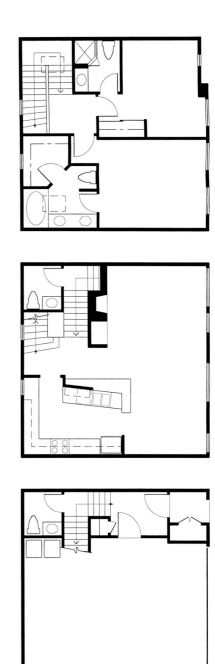

opposite top left Interior atrium offers protected space
opposite bottom left Three-story townhouse plan
opposite bottom right Three-story block unit plan
below Atrium delivers light from above
right top Kitchen offers view to entertaining area
right bottom Interiors are light, and flow
photography Tom Rider

Summit at Brighton

Rochester, New York
DiMella Shaffer Associates

The 25-acre site for this new continuing-care retirement community presented a great challenge to the design team. To the north was a major highway and to the east a six-story nursing facility. The existing terrain was flat with almost no vegetation and had a natural water table only one foot below grade.

The design solution includes the creation of three ponds to provide a focus for views from the apartments and common areas, while also controlling the unusually high water table. These ponds now attract a variety of wildlife, including ducks and geese. In addition, the land was molded and planted to create buffers to the adjacent highway and the nursing facility. The placement of the buildings in the landscape is purposefully casual, not unlike a loose collection of farm buildings indigenous to the area.

The design for the community pivots around a single-story tent-like structure, which serves as the central commons. This space includes all the social areas for the independent community and provides the central kitchen for the adjoining assisted-living building. The residential buildings and a new fitness center are joined to the commons by glass and brick single-story connecting links, which encourage views to the outdoors. Honey-colored brick with contrasting precast white sills and dark green, metal-clad wood windows were selected as exterior materials to maximize the reflective quality of the light on the brick surfaces, even on overcast days. Consequently, even the snowiest days are "sunny."

The two-story assisted-living building provides for 30 residents in efficiency and one-bedroom units, as well as all the common areas for this more frail population. The quality and design of this building is similar in nature to the independent commons building.

In order to allow residents to age in place, the entire building is accessible. The common areas are conveniently and centrally located to encourage use by residents. Lean rails are utilized in corridors as subtle assists to residents if they tire during walking. All units have large accessible bathrooms with showers and easily accessible kitchens.

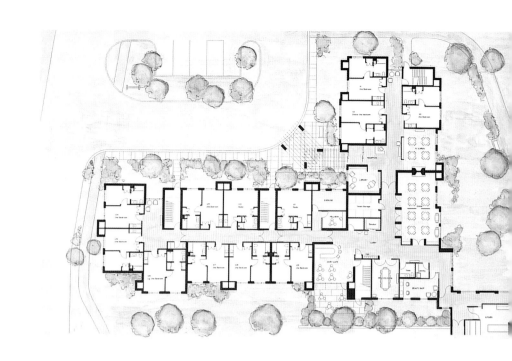

opposite   Site model
top   Site plan of one wing
middle left Buildings scaled to natural surroundings
middle right Natural features accentuate exterior
left   Warmth of brick used extensively

TERRACE
14'-4"x6'-6"

MECH.

DINING
8'-11"x8'-1"

BATHROOM
7'-8"x5'-6"

KITCHEN
8'-6"x7'-6"

DW

R

LIVING
11'-0"x19'-8"

BEDROOM
11'-0"x11'-6"

W/D

L

L

BEDROOM
13'-0"x12'-0"

BATHROOM
6'-0"x9'-7"

15'-3 1/4"

26'-0"

8'-4"

26'-2"

Willow
Chicago, Illinois
Pappageorge/Haymes Architects
Court

A railroad-switching yard in the heart of Chicago's Bucktown neighborhood was converted into the Willow Court townhome complex. A 20-foot rise from one end of the site to the other created by the abutment of an infrequently used railroad line posed a particularly difficult challenge. This grade change was kept and the existing retaining wall was modified to allow pedestrian access to the courtyards throughout the complex.

The site design staggers the homes, creating interest while minimizing their impact. Siting the units in this way also allowed the opportunity to create landscaped courtyards with gateways to the homes behind.

A long access drive extends through the site, off of which are found individual unit driveways. These surfaces are paved in brick and landscaped to soften the environment. Three-hour-rated demising walls were systemized through the unique application of industrial precast concrete wall panels, reducing both the project's cost and construction time.

The architecture is strongly vertical and expressive of its powerful massing, yet sensitive, to contribute a comfortable human scale. Large, black steel cantilevered bays at the block corners provided expansive views and light. Two colors of brick emphasize the design's form and massing. The body of the complex is rendered in a light-colored buff brick, while vertical bays are expressed in a darker brown material. The black metal window sash is refined and elegant. Each of the 56 units is capped with a penthouse terrace that offers spectacular views of the city.

opposite News façades punctuated with balconies
   right Different colors of brick distinquish elevations
   below Dark materials anchor building corners

below left   Back of units face each other across a mews
below right   Detail of steel sash windows used throughout
opposite top   Detail of brick and steel façades
opposite bottom   Forms fill out site to street edge

opposite top   Typical unit kitchen interior
opposite bottom   Interior view from dining to living areas
below   Interiors are light and spacious
photography   Pappageorge/Haymes

Twenty

Toronto, Ontario
architects Alliance

Niagra

Situated beside Victoria Memorial Park in Toronto's warehouse district, Twenty Niagara was the first new development to be built under the City of Toronto's new King/Spadina zoning by-law, which encouraged the redevelopment of the King-Spadina industrial district. Twenty is intended as a new housing type that realizes greater density without sacrificing the domestic ideals that are important to the city.

The building contains 20 single-loaded "through units" designed in the loft style, with 10-foot ceilings, exposed concrete walls, and large expanses of windows. Each suite opens onto a private terrace or balcony overlooking the park and city skyline to the east, and Lake Ontario to the south.

Twenty combines two of the innovative building forms typical of the Modern movement—the arrangement of vertically-stacked units around a central circulation core, and the exterior walkway—in a way that augments the benefits and minimizes the shortcomings of each.

The vertical core has not found wide application in North America; building code requirements for two separate exits have instead resulted in the widespread construction of slab buildings with double-loaded corridors. Single-loaded walkway schemes (most common in Britain) fail to provide adequate privacy, and are not ideally suited to the Toronto climate. The architects were able to arrive at a viable combination of these forms by rethinking the building's circulation and life-safety issues.

Through the elimination of the typical internal corridor, each apartment acquires a dual aspect, with the front of each suite facing east onto Victoria Memorial Park. This provides greater ventilation and light penetration, and enables residents to share in the amenity of the public park. It also preserves the clarity of orientation that characterizes most of Toronto's residential neighborhoods.

Two separate elevators, each serving two suites per floor, provide the principal point of access and eliminate the need for a public corridor. The secondary exit required by the building code is provided at the rear of the building via a linear exterior walkway—a reinterpretation of the traditional fire escape.

opposite   Building as it faces east with view of park
right   Exterior detail of sunroom
below   East elevation at night reveals volumes

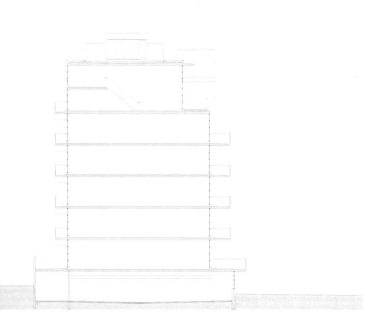

opposite top   Section
opposite bottom   Detail of glass and concrete structure
below   South elevation as it faces Niagra

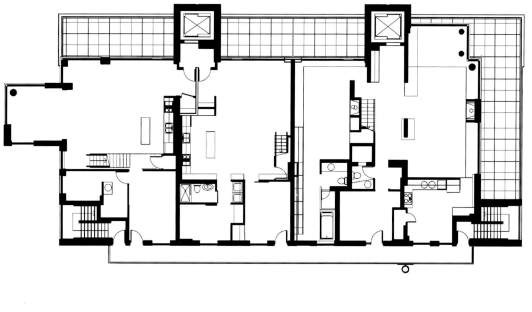

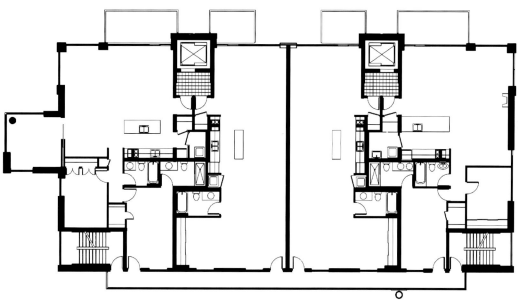

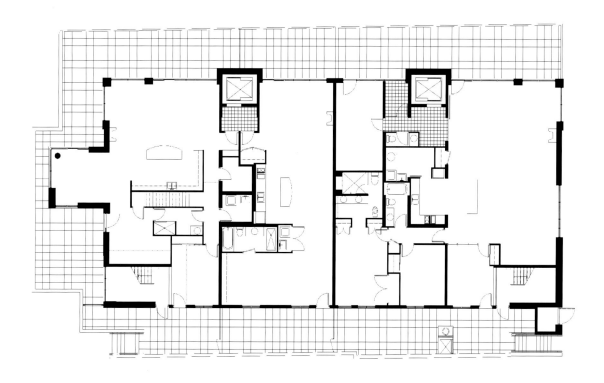

Austin Shoal Creek

Austin, Texas
RTKL

Located along three acres of land near Shoal Creek and adjacent to a future light rail, this 239-unit residential community offers easy access to Austin's hike and bike trail, the West 6th Street retail district, Whole Foods' flagship store, and the popular warehouse entertainment and dining areas. The community promotes the live/work concept, with part of the ground floor accommodating offices and shops.

This residential neighborhood embraces the rich cultural influences of the surrounding area by acknowledging Shoal Creek on one side and the rail yard on the other. A "tree house" tower overlooks the creek, featuring an outdoor community room with Austin stone walls at its base, and provides a memorable image from West Avenue. The rail-yard side of the project features a "loading dock" character, with a corrugated metal canopy covering live/work units faced with glazed garage doors that can be raised in good weather. Building massing was established by a view corridor to the state capitol dome, so that the project appears to be a series of smaller buildings that have been built over time and fit easily into the context. Shoal Creek's earthy colors and bright accents lend an air of sophistication and reflect the warmth of the Texas climate.

The community offers 60 unique floor plans, including lofts. Apartments feature hardwood and polished concrete floors, varied ceiling heights, balconies/patios and always-on high-speed Internet access. Among the community amenities are pools, a fitness center, business center, courtyard fireplaces, roof-top deck, and covered or garage parking.

opposite left   Four-story wing as it faces the street
opposite right   Project forms a street edge
below left   Units as they face the street
below right   Warm colors used on façades
bottom   Project in its urban context

opposite left   Pedestrian paths surround complex
opposite right   Bright colors on parking garage
below   Site plan
bottom left   Units as they surround the pool
bottom middle   Tree house tower overlooks the creek
bottom right   Pedestrian paths next to units
photography   David Whitcomb

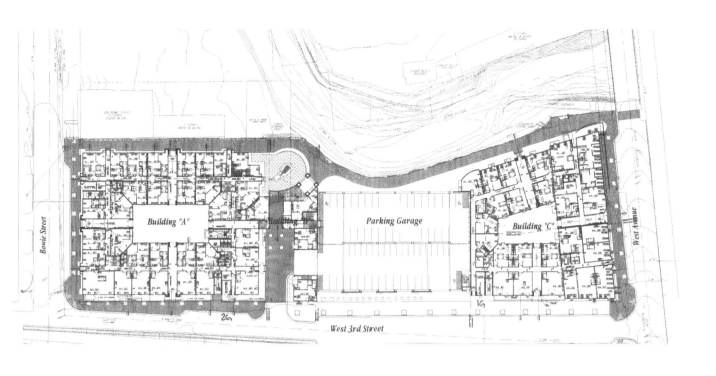

Hilltop Suites

University of Connecticut , Storrs, Connecticut
Herbert S. Newman and Partners

This 140,000-square-foot residence hall provides 450 beds for the campus. The new design encloses a quadrangle with house-like forms to give the architecture an intimate residential scale. The program includes a large conference facility, a main common lounge on the main floor, smaller lounges on each of the four floors, and a laundry facility in the basement.

The building backs onto an athletic field, turning inward to create a protected, welcoming entry courtyard. The building wraps the courtyard on three sides, creating an outdoor "room" that provides the student community with an important place for gathering. The wings that reach out to define the courtyard are topped with gable-roofed forms that suggest "home." This courtyard is also visually secure, in that half the suites in the building look out onto it. At the very end of the wings, on each of the four above-ground levels, are small lounge areas for study and socializing. The "elbows" of the building's arms also contain lounge spaces that offer views out over the campus. Near the building entrance is a large social space with an enclosed mezzanine level, suitable for meetings, parties, and other small gatherings.

Except for resident advisory rooms and a sprinkling of single suites, the majority of accommodations in the building are double suites, arranged on double-loaded corridors. Lounge spaces anchor the corridors and provide much-welcomed natural light. The suites themselves are spacious with large windows and a combination of private and semi-private areas.

opposite   Entry to dormitory at night
right   Building backs up onto athletic field
below   Gable roof forms communicate a sense of "home"

opposite   Main entrance is open and light-filled
   right   Building entry court can be easily seen from rooms
   below   Ground floor plan

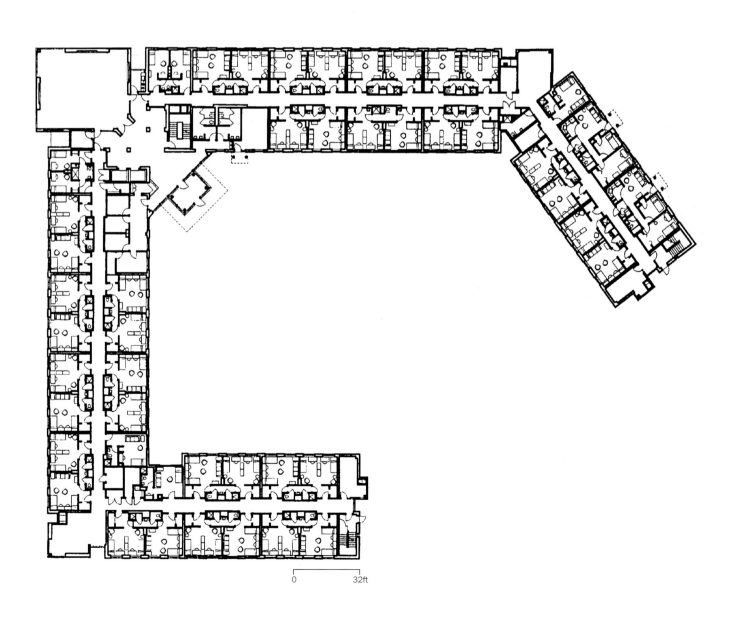

0   32ft

opposite   Large lounge on entry floor
below   View from second floor into entry-level lounge
bottom   Lounge areas offer views of surrounding campus
photography Robert Benson

Park Place

Mountain View, California
Seidel/Holzman Architecture, Project Architect
Sandy & Babcock International, Architect of Record

South

Park Place South is a high-density residential block fronting Castro Street and located within easy walking distance of the city's new public amenities. In keeping with the retail character of Castro Street, the first level of the project contains shops. Restaurants spill out onto a wide sidewalk with café seating.

Three large mature redwood trees are preserved in a courtyard facing Castro Street, recalling the heritage of the site as the former location of the Mountain View High School. The courtyard also leads to a pedestrian stair that enters the second level residential courtyard. Three levels of flats and townhouses are entered from the courtyard, with each apartment having its own exterior entry. Landscaping and brick paving create a cloistered feeling in the courtyard.

The architecture expresses Park Place's residential character, while being compatible with adjacent commercial structures. The white stucco and gray metal roofs recall the materials of the office building to the north, and the two buildings jointly define a pedestrian path that leads through the site to Eagle Park, one block off of Castro Street.

The building becomes tower-like at the intersection of the path and Castro Street. Parking is handled on several different levels. Retail parking is at grade but only within the center of the block so that it is screened by retail or residential uses on all four sides. Another below-grade parking level extends to the entire footprint of the block, accommodating adequate parking for the 120 residential units.

Park Place's high 85-unit-per-acre density does not sacrifice the enhanced urban amenities for its residents, including retail shops, open space courts, and passages that weave it into the larger fabric of its community.

below left   Retail uses are found at grade street level
below right   Elevation along Castro Street
opposite   Gated residential entry

opposite   Courtyard is a protected space
below   Site plan, residential countyard
right   Complex has comfortable urban scale
bottom   Ground floor plan
photography   Jay Graham

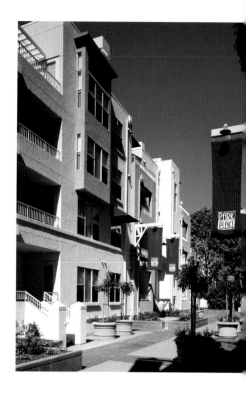

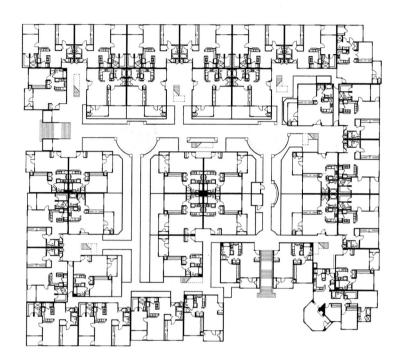

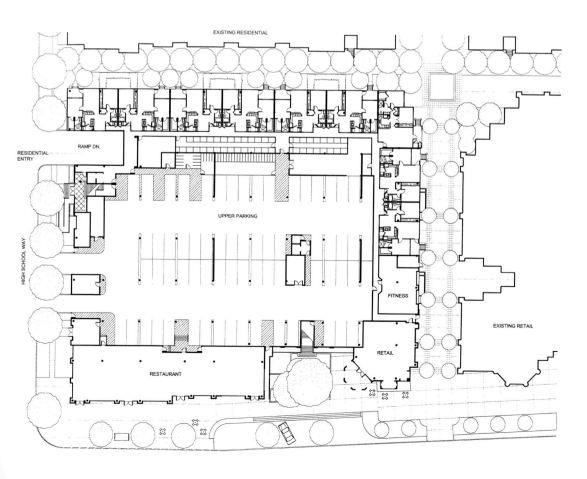

EXISTING RESIDENTIAL

RESIDENTIAL ENTRY

RAMP DN.

HIGH SCHOOL WAY

UPPER PARKING

FITNESS

EXISTING RETAIL

RETAIL

RESTAURANT

Park
West

Charlotte, North Carolina
David Furman Architecture

The programmatic task was to create as many affordable units as possible while maintaining a sensitive residential scale on this 1.8-acre infill site. The efficient rowhouse layout incorporates 30 units between 1,050 and 1,400 square feet, or about 16.6 units per acre.

The site is located behind a street-front development on a major traffic corridor. Therefore, all units are accessed internally from surface parking and orient onto private courtyards behind each dwelling. Courtyards are walled to foster privacy without the loss of views. The units are arranged in long buildings that face onto the internalized parking. There is a mixture of two- and three-story pods to ensure diversity of massing as well as unit size and price. The tight site plan ensures that private and public exterior areas are appropriately scaled to foster a sense of community and security within the neighborhood.

The interiors of the units are open to maximize the sense of space, given their rather modest square footage. In the spirit of the rowhouse layout the units are narrow, yet are flooded with light on both ends of the plan through generous fenestration. Living spaces flow between distinct areas for entertaining, dining, food preparation, and family relaxation. Generous bedrooms and bathrooms distinguish the second floor.

Exteriors are all wood siding and trim on wood-frame buildings, with crisp detailing. The materials and their colors create an alternative to the more traditional builder offerings that dominate the marketplace. The unique aesthetic, affordable pricing, and in-fill location resulted in a quick sell-out.

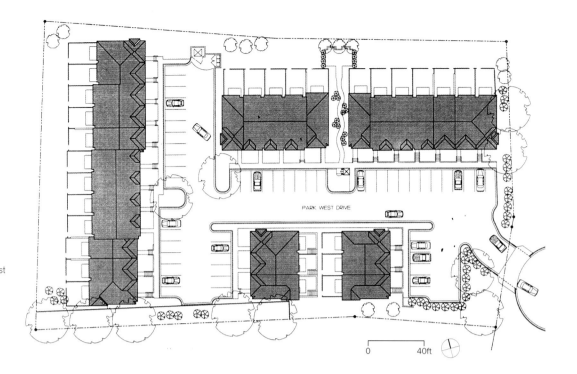

PARK WEST DRIVE

0   40ft

opposite left   Window treatments create interest
opposite right   Units are slightly held back from
                  street edge
right   Site plan
below   Unit entries have a comfortable
         domestic scale

Gateway
Commons

Emeryville, California
Pyatok Architects

Located on a 30-mile-long boulevard that passes through six cities, this derelict site became the focus of neighborhood protest and activism because of drug dealing and a poorly managed liquor store. The neighbors in this low-income, racially diverse neighborhood succeeded in closing down the liquor store and securing the site for development by a non-profit corporation. The site is divided among three jurisdictions—two cities on each side of an underground creek owned by the county. It became the focus of six participatory neighborhood design workshops during which four teams of neighbors, using 3-D modeling kits supplied by the architect, explored options for developing the site.

The result of the workshops was a combination of 17 homes for low- and moderate-income first-time homebuyers arranged in two rows around a central auto-pedestrian court. Each unit has the potential to include a home-based business. The neighbors recognized no one would buy a house on such a busy street unless they needed to because they maintained a home-based business on the ground floor. On the other hand, they also realized that not all buyers would want to maintain a home business. Hence the dwellings facing the street have a double-height flexible front room and entry from the street so that it can be used as a business; a front "outdoor patio room" acts as an acoustical and privacy buffer from the busy street if the occupants want to use the room for residential purposes.

The back row of units, since they do not have street exposure, were provided their "business opportunity" by placing a bedroom with its own half-bath and plumbing stub-outs for a drop-in kitchen so that the room could be used as an accessory rental unit with access to the rear yard. All units have outdoor decks above their garages entered from their kitchen-dining rooms. The central driveway is paved as a pedestrian court and is intended as a play area. Landscape open space was located where the creek passes under the site.

opposite   Development as it faces San Pablo Avenue
left   Site plan
below left   San Pablo Avenue façade faces west
below right   Detail of 48th Street façades
bottom left   Gate affording center of development privacy
bottom right   Color and form articulate development

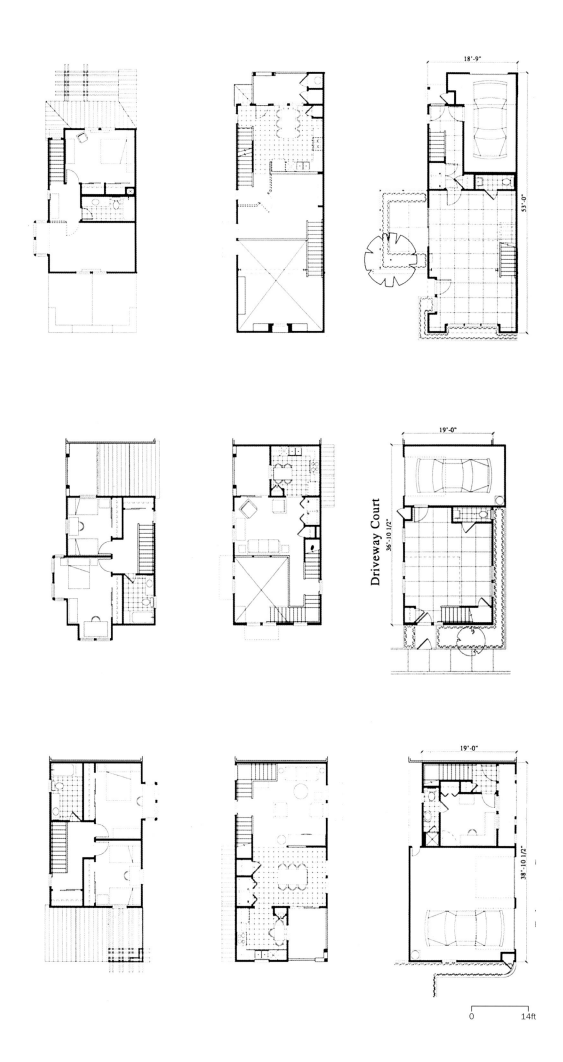

Driveway Court

18'-9"

53'-0"

19'-0"

36'-10 1/2"

19'-0"

38'-10 1/2"

0   14ft

138

opposite top   San Pablo Avenue unit plans
opposite middle   48th Street unit plans
opposite bottom   Mews corner unit plans
right   Interior of living space in unit
below   Detailing of west-facing façade
bottom   Auto-pedestrian court provides access to units
photography   Pyatok Architects

Atlanta, Georgia
Brock Green Architects

15 Waddell

This 18,000-square-foot condominium project is steeped in the spirit of early Modern architecture of the 1920s. Located in Atlanta's historically industrial area of Inman Park, the 15-unit development is highly expressive of its concrete construction technique. These units are designed to invoke a machine aesthetic of European Modernism while providing all of the conveniences of contemporary living.

The three-story building occupies a tight rectangular form. Eroded portions of the concrete box reveal wood-clad elements. The project utilizes a unique cost-effective tilt-up concrete panel construction technique that serves as the background plane from which balconies project and portions of the plan shift in and out. The tilt-up construction is most clearly seen on the east elevation, which faces the parking lot. Window slits were integrated into the tilt-up walls to provide framed views of the downtown skyline. The warmth of stained cypress wood siding contrasts with the machine-like precision of the concrete panels.

In order to provide the open "loft" atmosphere within a tight footprint, large openings of combined plate glass and thin glass block panel systems were used. The interiors of the units are light, airy, and spacious, with exposed mechanical ducts and warm wood floors. Within each bathroom round frosted windows deliver generous natural light without sacrificing privacy.

The roof plane is supported by continuous steel columns that run from the ground to the roof, and expresses a continuous edge around the building's perimeter. The fire stair is pulled outside of the overall box form and is exposed as a structural element.

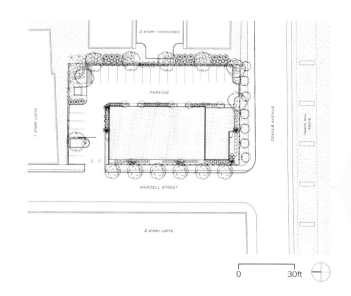

0   30ft

opposite left   East elevation expresses tilt-up concrete panel construction
opposite right   Site plan
right   Detail of unit balcony
below   Building from the southwest, with eroded form

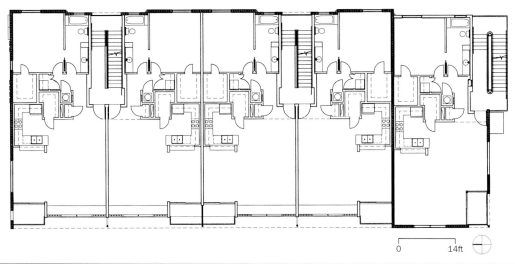

0   14ft

opposite top   Second and third floor plan
opposite bottom   Spacious unit interiors are filled with light
right   Transverse section
below   Units feature glass-block windows and clear glass
photography   Rebecca Bockman

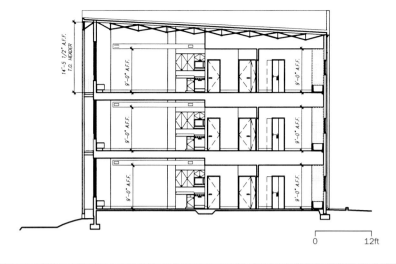

0   12ft

143

Riverwatch

New York, New York
Hardy Holzman Pfeiffer Associates

Riverwatch, located off of the area's South Cove, is one of the few remaining sites to be developed in New York's Battery Park City at the foot of Manhattan. This multifamily project was developed with 70 percent of the apartments to be sold at market value, and the remaining 30 percent to be offered by lottery to low-income households.

Riverwatch enjoys an ideal site for urban living. It fronts Battery Place between Second and Third Places, offering views of the Hudson River. This nine-story building contains a total of 209 apartments, comprised of five three-bedroom units, 89 two-bedroom units, 105 one-bedroom units, and 10 studio apartments. The building occupies a U-shaped footprint, with the inside of the shape devoted to a public courtyard behind the project. This amenity, which can be viewed from the apartment wings that surround it, offers residents a green respite in the city.

The exterior of the building recalls the tradition of apartment house design in Manhattan. The front façade is placed along the street edge to reinforce the urban density of the neighborhood. This façade is articulated with glassy bay windows that allow residents views up and down the street, as well as toward the river. Corner windows maximize sunlight in the units. The building features a granite watercourse and rusticated limestone at its base, while taupe- and buff-colored brick form the bulk of the building's exterior. A detailed cornice crowns Riverwatch. The public lobby is rendered in cool, dark colors, lending an air of refinement and sophistication.

opposite	Building as it defines a courtyard at the rear
below left	Front façade at street level
below right	Corner windows accentuate light and views
bottom left	Generous lobby space greets residents and visitors
bottom right	Lobby is welcoming and refined with dark wood
photography	Chris Lovi

1500
Orange Place

Escondido, California
Studio E Architects

Thirty-two one-, two-, three-, and four-bedroom townhouse units stretch along this long, thin site on a small street in the older section of Escondido. The units are grouped to form edges and make useable, defined outdoor spaces in the tradition of Southern California's bungalow courts. Three separate courtyards are formed; the center one contains commons areas for the entire project. These areas include a meeting hall, outdoor terrace, tot lot, and garden plots.

Alternating between the "people" spaces are automobile courts of a manageable scale. Each of these courts is treated as a bosque of trees and thought of as landscape areas that also happen to function for the storage of cars.

The individual units extend the site strategy of courtyards by organizing around an outdoor room. These spaces are shaded with pull-back fabric awnings. Enclosed on three sides, these spaces flow out from the interior living room and mitigate between inside and public courtyard spaces.

The units themselves are sensitively scaled and offer a variety of familiar forms and colors, all very much at home in the Southern California context.

The playful forms grow from balconies, covered trellis areas, shed roofs, and low-walled courtyards. The complex is extremely pedestrian friendly, fostering a sense of a close-knit neighborhood. Exterior materials are simple stucco, wood, and metal siding, with generous overhangs that provide shade from the sun.

The interiors are simply detailed, open, light, and spacious, with views through layers of space to outdoor living precincts. Large windows and modestly scaled interiors mean that the living spaces are flooded with natural light. Structural expression inside can be seen through exposed wood beams.

left   Interiors are light and connected to outdoor space
above   Sensitive scale of townhouses
opposite top left   Axonometric of typical unit
opposite top right   Three- and four-bedroom unit floor plan
opposite bottom left   Townhouses use a variety of materials
opposite bottom right   View of courtyard space
photography   Courtesy of architect

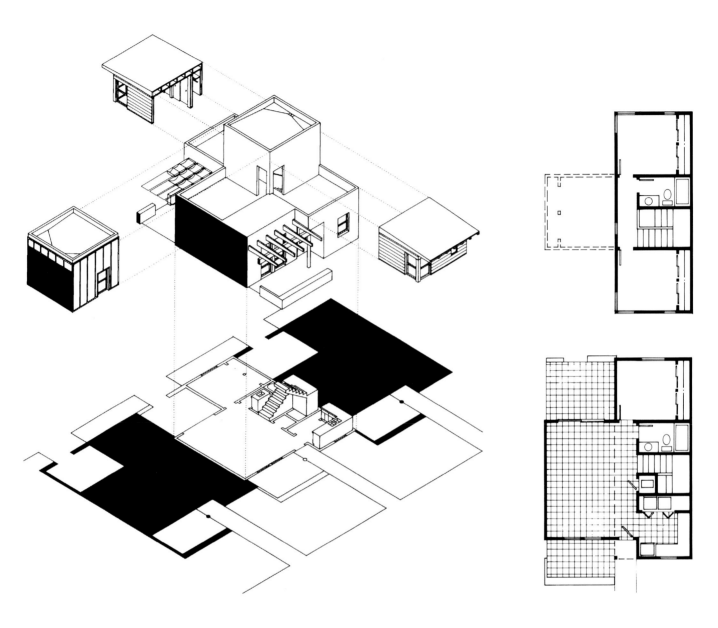

King Farm

Rockville, Maryland
Torti Gallas and Partners

Apartments

The King Farm development is an innovative mix of high and low-density apartment living in a traditional neighborhood design. The buildings in this apartment neighborhood front the streets, forming traditional streetscapes consistent with the vision of the King Farm master plan. In addition, the buildings form interior spaces with a system of alleys providing access to individual rear-loaded garages.

The King Farm development encompasses a total of 402 units distributed throughout 32 buildings, configured in four types of units. There are 176 garden apartments in six buildings. With a total site area of just less than 13 acres, this number of units encourages a close-knit neighborhood, which is a hallmark of traditional neighborhood design.

In creating a diverse streetscape similar to those found in traditional neighborhoods, three distinct unit types form the lower density portion of the project. Combinations of the Townhouse (three-story, single unit) and the Charleston House (triplex, three-story unit) form the "body" of the streetscape. The Townhouse is a common type found in this part of the country.

The Charleston House model is a variant on the "single-house" type that is native to Charleston, South Carolina, noted for their side porches, which encourage natural cooling. The Manor House, inspired by larger corner homes, consists of nine units on three floors. This building anchors the block corners of the primary street intersections.

The Garden apartments, on the northwest quadrant of the site, form green courtyards and are uniquely situated around a four-story concrete parking garage, which affords direct access to each level of the apartment building.

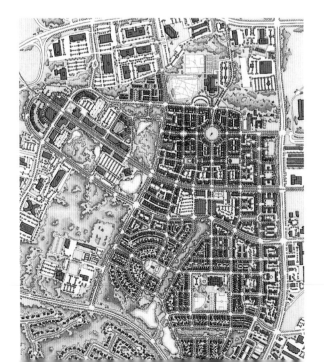

left   Overall community plan
photography   Torti Gallas and Partners
opposite top left   Charleston House units have side porches
opposite top right   Density of units contributes community appeal
opposite bottom   Charleston House units are sensitively scaled
photography   Richard Robinson

Parkview

San Jose, California
Sandy & Babcock International

Senior Apartments

Part of a full-block master plan designed to revitalize a former industrial area, this project provides much needed affordable senior housing for the City of San Jose. The developer of the project was the Ecumenical Association for Housing. This project's senior housing component is mixed with affordable family housing and townhouses, which are located on separate sub-parcels. The three components are sited along a pedestrian promenade, which leads to a new retail center. The three housing types are linked by courtyards, designed to encourage interaction between residents of all ages and income levels within the overall project.

The 140 low-income senior apartments are housed in four-story buildings, clustered around a private and secure courtyard. The courtyard serves as a green heart for the project, and units look out over this outdoor space from balconies. The courtyard features a trellis and ample places to sit and relax. The project has a density of 39 units per acre.

Each floor has a "parlor" or "living room" for socializing, in addition to the ground floor community meeting and recreational facilities. The architecture is clean and simple, yet a muted color palette, careful detailing, stepped elevations, and inset balconies soften the mid-rise design. The lush plantings help modulate the human scale of the complex. Even though this project has a fairly high density, landscaping, natural light, and the massing of the buildings all contribute a sense that Parkview is less populated than it actually is.

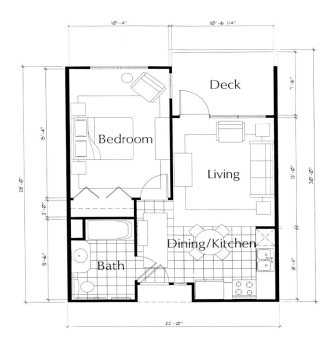

top right   Typical unit floor plan
right   Courtyard offers a protected place for sitting and socializing
opposite top   First floor plan
opposite bottom   Colors and shaded setbacks enliven façades
Photography   Jay Graham

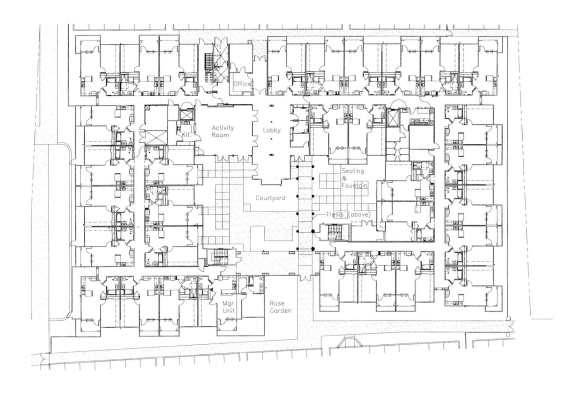

Block 588

Dallas, Texas
RTKL

Located in the historic State Thomas District near downtown Dallas, Block 588 consists of 127 two-story loft units providing a total of 230,000 square feet of space. The residential development creates a loft-warehouse character appropriate to its urban context, and takes advantage of both park and downtown views. The exterior materials relate well to the neighborhood's urban character—brick, steel, wire mesh, metal window frames, unfinished concrete—lending it an uncompromisingly gutsy appearance. A yellow tubular steel brace supporting the roof at the penthouse level is another example of how this building flexes its muscles. It also gives Block 588 a landmark signature in Dallas.

The five-story building's U-shaped plan helps to define a courtyard, with units oriented to overlook either it or the city skyline. All residences, including the four penthouses that survey downtown Dallas, are two-story mezzanine units with 19-foot ceilings. The interiors feature exposed concrete, wood floors, and exposed steel bar joist structures, which yield an authentic loft aesthetic. All residences have expansive floor-to-ceiling windows. On the curving south side, the balconies are shaded from the brutal Texas sun by the concrete structure. Visual privacy between the balconies is provided by simple corrugated metal screens, which fit into the loft-building aesthetic.

Below-grade parking accommodates 143 cars and creates a base for a street-side courtyard and terrace for residents. The courtyard is rendered with flair. Tile patterning on the courtyard floor lends an illusion of depth, and provides some visual sophistication when seen from the units that overlook it.

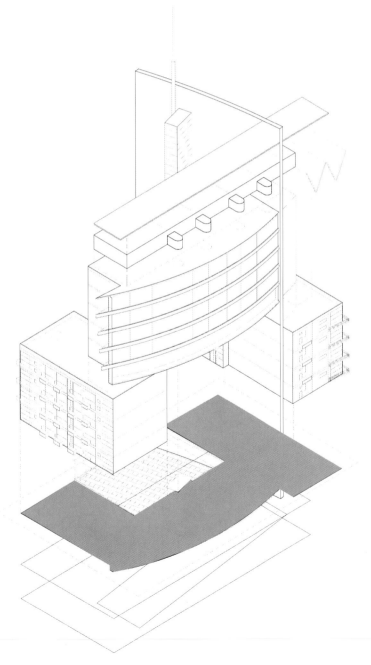

left Axonometric
opposite top Curved wall opens units to views
opposite bottom Detail of south elevation

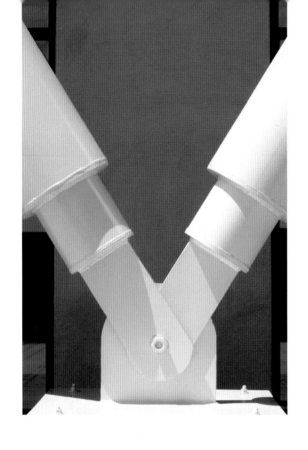

left   Detail of roof brace
below   East elevation with distinctive brace
opposite top left   First floor plan
opposite top right   Second floor plan
opposite bottom   East elevation distinguished by balconies

154

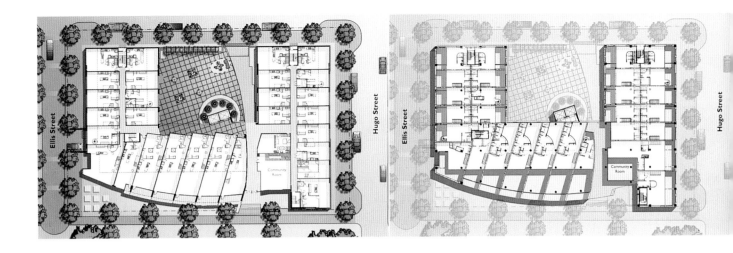

155

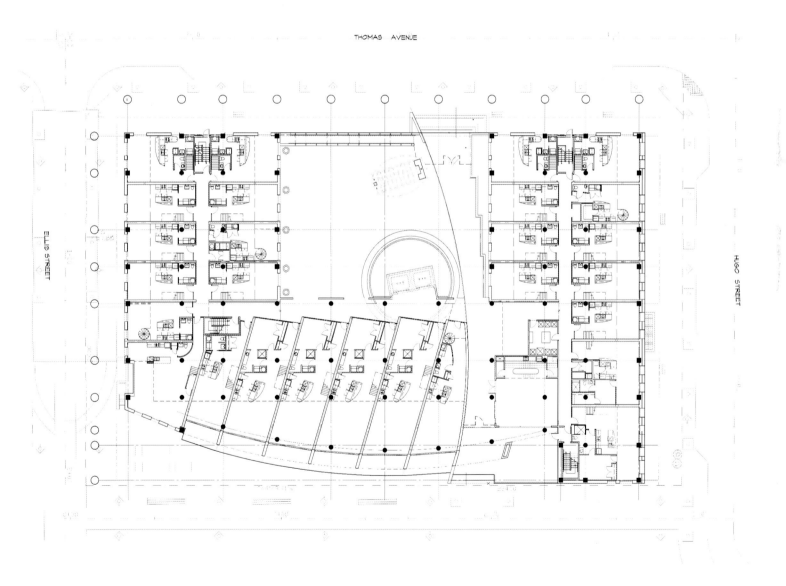

City Life
Courtyard Housing

Portland, Oregon, USA
Ellen Fortin and Michael Tingley, Design Architects
Robertson, Merryman, Barnes Architects, Architect of Record

This project is the winning entry for courtyard housing in a design competition for affordable, innovative urban housing, built by a nonprofit developer. The project goals were to demonstrate market viability, affordability, design compatibility, and innovative architectural design for inner-city medium-density housing. The design strategy for the site addresses its edge condition: a light industrial zone to the east, and a more traditional early-20th century single-family residential neighborhood surrounding the remainder of the site.

The 10 housing units are organized as two interlocking L-shaped bars with the courtyard as a focal point for the residents. Along the street the housing units are two stories, maximizing light in the courtyard. This housing bar is broken into segments by several circulation paths to the court, allowing movement and views between the courtyard and the street, with a scale more compatible with the nearby single-family homes. Along the alley, three-story units form a buffer to the courtyard from the industrial area.

The courtyard is the organizing element of this project, representing the idea of community and providing the project's identity. The courtyard is an interactive middle ground between public and private realms, giving each unit a large open space. Shaped by subtle deformations in the orientation of the surrounding buildings, there is an intentional casual quality to the plan. The courtyard is a place of potential, assigned many values; a secret garden, a place of informal gathering, the threshold to a small community.

The compact housing units have interiors with unexpected sectional variety and a rich material palette, including exposed wood ceilings. Analogous to the simplicity of the nautilus shell, movement through the units leads to greater levels of privacy. The street units orient to both the street and the courtyard, participating in the life of both realms. The alley units are organized to orient to the courtyard. Unlike the rowhouse typology, the units are oriented with the long exposure to the street and court to maximize on light and views.

1 STORY
BUILDING

First Floor Plan - Unit Type 3

First Floor Plan - Unit Type 1

KITCHEN
DINING ROOM
LIVING ROOM

DINING ROOM
LIVING ROOM

KITCHEN
DINING ROOM

Second Floor Plan - Unit Type 1

LAUNDRY
BEDROOM 1
BEDROOM 2
HALL

S.E. Sixteenth Avenue

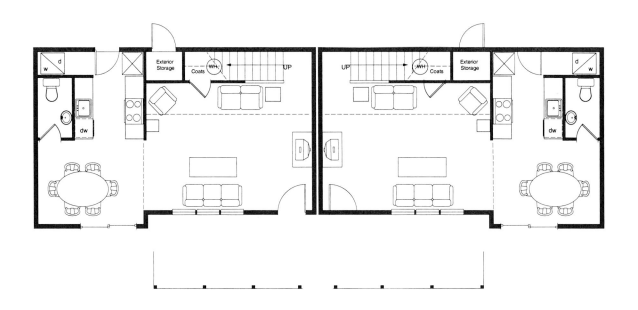

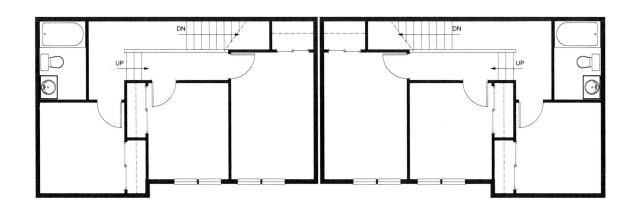

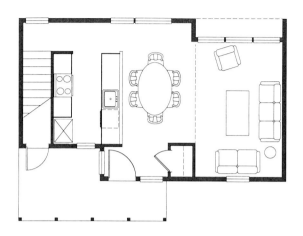

161

Swans Market

Oakland, California
Pyatok Architects

The Swans Market is a mixed-use renovation of the existing historic Swans Market Building, a major shopping destination for all of the East Bay for over 60 years. The existing structure, built in several stages between 1917 and 1940, encompasses an entire city block in the Old Oakland Neighborhood.

The façade is a beautiful example of glazed brick and terra cotta commercial architecture, and includes polychrome terra cotta medallions depicting the fresh foods available in the Market Hall.

The open interiors are flooded with natural light thanks to 200-foot-long, north-facing clerestories supported by long-span steel trusses.

The renovation of this historic downtown destination by the nonprofit East Bay Asian Local Development Corporation is the key element in the City of Oakland's attempt to shape a new residential neighborhood downtown. The project includes 20 cohousing units and a common house, 18 affordable one- and two-bedroom rental units, live/work space, a fresh food market hall, street-oriented retail and restaurants, sidewalk dining, commercial space, and on-site parking. The Museum of Children's Art occupies a second floor space overlooking Swans Court and sponsors indoor and outdoor projects for children on site.

Most of the existing structure (80 percent) is retained, including the existing terra cotta and glazed brick façade. A new three-story wood-framed building clad in tile and cement plaster continues the character of the existing buildings. Portions of the existing roof are peeled away to bring sunlight into the interior of the block and to create public and semi-private outdoor spaces that link the diverse uses into a vibrant, unique urban community, attracting new residents and patrons to this resurgent neighborhood.

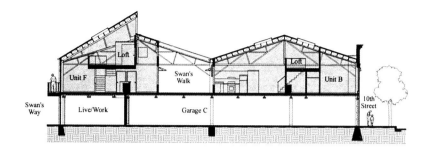

opposite   Colorful awnings articulate façade
top   Section
middle left   Project as it faces 9th Street
middle right   Courtyard provides protected interior space
above left   Courtyard meanders through center of community
above right   Trusses span over courtyard space

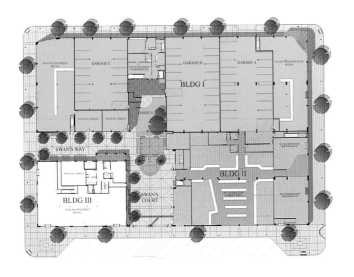

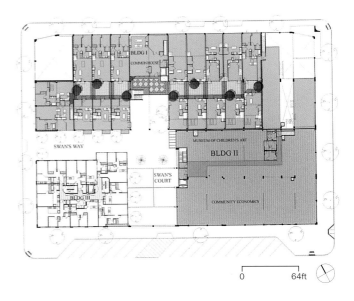

0   64ft

top left	Ground floor plan
top right	Second floor plan
above left	Swans Walk is carefully scaled and domestic
above right	Interior of common house space
photography	Pyatok Architects
opposite top	Café space is light and airy
photography	Russell Abraham
opposite bottom left	Common house features generous fenestration
photography	Pyatok Architects
opposite bottom right	Spaces are enlivened with truss structure above
photography	Russell Abraham

Post Uptown Place

Charlotte, North Carolina
David Furman Architecture

The resurgence of the American city as a viable place to not only work, but also live, has created a significant opportunity for new mixed-use housing projects. These projects must work towards the community mission of creating active and animated streets that encourage and relate to the pedestrian.

The block that this development occupies is divided conceptually into two parts. The first is a five-story building with an industrial flavor, with ground-level shops, which front onto North Graham Street (a busy, high-traffic corridor). This structure wraps a five-level concrete-deck parking garage, which is more economical than sub-surface parking.

The parking deck is surrounded by wood and metal-frame residential construction, totally hiding it from the street. Units in this building have loft-like open plans. The building's upper corner, which orients toward the Uptown Charlotte skyline, is eroded to create a roof terrace.

The second part is a four-story building with two levels of flats stacked on townhouses located below. The townhouses have access through front-entry doors with stoops at street level.

The stoops help to encourage pedestrian traffic and to activate the side streets, which have a much more residential character than North Graham Street. The interior of the block is a multi-level courtyard with pools, fountains, and landscaping. The two buildings take on different aesthetics to look less like a project and more like the evolution of the block. Exterior materials consist of brick, concrete block, and stucco.

The density achieved through the design is 90 units per acre, which totals 227 units on this site. The apartments range in size from 510 to 1,600 square feet.

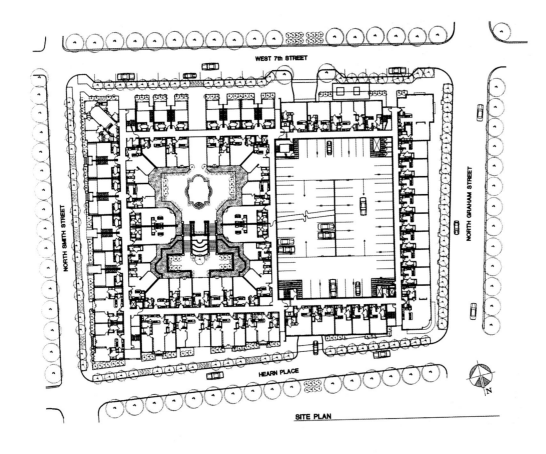

SITE PLAN

opposite   Site plan
left   Building anchors the corner
below left   Turret expresses the corner
below right   Details at top of building lend character

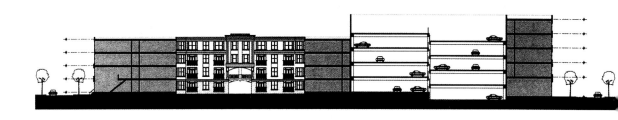

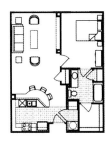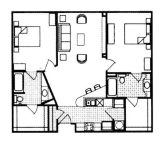

top Section
middle Typical unit plans
left Interiors have figural elements
opposite top right Gazebo is a welcome amenity
opposite bottom left Courtyard offers respite from urban context
opposite bottom right Units are scaled for urban presence
photography Tim Buchman

168

Palo Alto, California
Seidel/Holzman Architecture

Montage

Palo Alto is in the process of rezoning and reorienting El Camino Real, the major north-south artery in the community. Characterized by typical strip retail with on-grade parking, the city wishes to create more pedestrian-oriented, mixed-use development along the street.

Following in the wake of a community charette that identified housing as a major priority in this corridor, this residential project both intensifies the site use and provides a pedestrian orientation, compared to the one-story commercial use it replaced. Reflecting the goals of the plan, this project creates a well-scaled elevation with pedestrian entrances in proximity to the street, and also forms a cloistered courtyard within the site to which each townhouse and flat has direct access.

The apartments are relatively small, and efficiently constructed so as to be attainable by the large university population in the community. The massing is playful and articulated with a variety of wood siding materials and colors to give distinction to individual apartments. The architectural character is conceived to relate to older eclectic residential neighborhoods to the west of the project and has been very well received by the community. The project is within easy walking distance of retail, restaurant and cultural facilities as well as the adjacent university.

All units are planned so that they have a minimum of two, and often three exposures for light and air. Many have multiple terraces and balconies. A number of townhouse units are included, a particularly attractive arrangement for multiple unrelated tenants who share accommodations during university associations.

The character of the architecture purposefully works with the agricultural heritage of the Santa Clara Valley, notable remnants of which still exist on nearby Stanford lands.

below   Roof shapes create a distinctive profile
opposite top   Site plan
opposite bottom   Stairs, porches, and balconies articulate façade

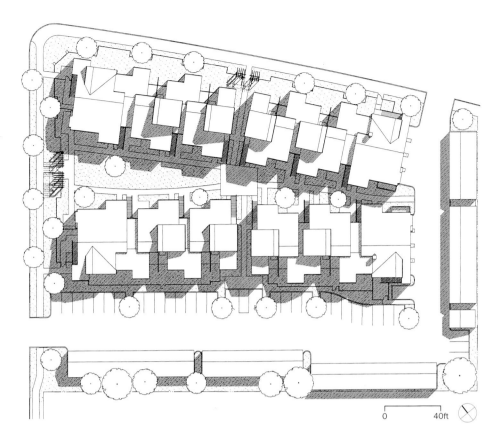

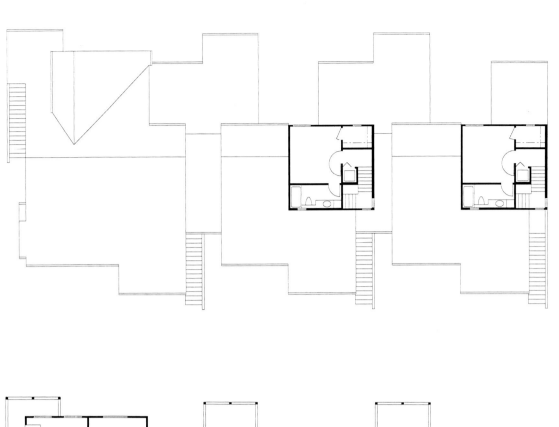

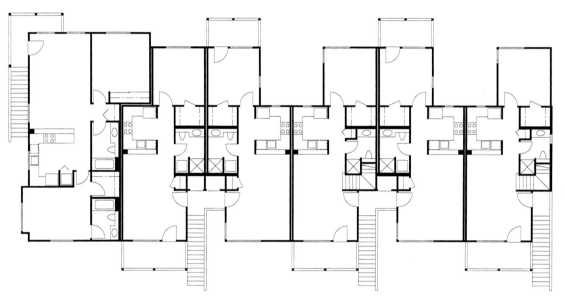

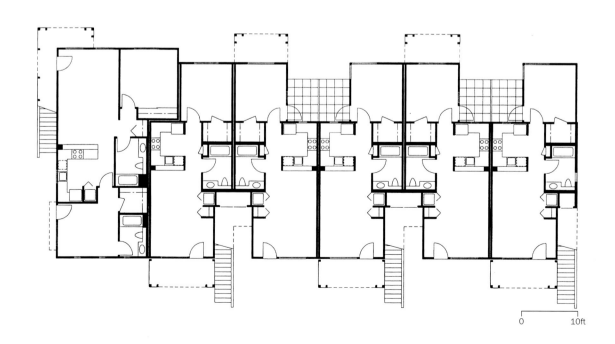

opposite top   Third floor plan
opposite middle   Second floor plan
opposite bottom   First floor plan
above left   Complex is scaled to the pedestrian
above right   Inner court provides privacy and quiet
below left   Units are expressed through exterior elements
below right   View between units into courtyard
photography   Tom Rider

Victoria Townhomes

Seattle, Washington
Mithun Architects

In Seattle's Queen Anne neighborhood, an early-1900s apartment building with inadequate on-site parking was slated for rehabilitation and conversion to condominiums. To supply an additional 60 parking spaces for the condominium conversion and to minimize the impact of a needed garage on the surrounding historic neighborhood, the design called for construction of a new, partially buried, two-level parking garage with housing above.

The original building and the condominium site are surrounded by two- and three-story masonry apartment buildings and historic, single-family detached homes. Neighborhood residents are affluent, politically active, and design conscious.

The architect led a review process involving the City Design Review Board, the Neighborhood Community Council, and the developer. The neighbors demonstrated support for the process. The result is 10 infill townhomes that blend seamlessly into the context. There is meticulous use of contextual exterior materials and colors. The units, which range from 2,200 to 2,400 square feet, have private entries and courtyards, with parking for both new and conversion units that is easily accessed and hidden below grade.

The careful use of roof forms, color, and materials is utilized to anchor the new project to the surrounding neighborhood. Although each townhome has an individual stair up from the parking garage, the relationship to the street was more important. Individual stairs to the street are designed into the parking garage base, each with its own gated entry. The project takes advantage of a generous right-of-way to the curb to provide almost all of the required landscaping for the project. By reducing the setbacks to the street and not building two separate buildings (as would have been required by zoning the new building), Victoria Townhomes knits together the surrounding fabric created by the older apartment blocks.

opposite   Site plan
left   Townhomes have an imposing street presence
below left   Units sit on stone bases
below right   Gable roofs communicate a domestic sensibility

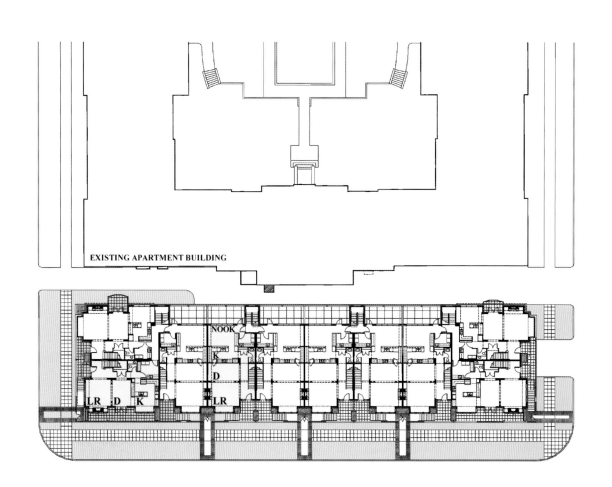

EXISTING APARTMENT BUILDING

NOOK

K

D

LR

LR D K

opposite top   Street elevation
opposite middle   Back elevation
opposite bottom   First floor plan
above left   Wood finishes warm compact kitchen
above right   Living spaces are light and airy
below   Kitchen has light-filled eating area
photography   Robert Pisano

Armitage/
Leavitt

Chicago, Illinois
Pappageorge/Haymes Architects

"Bold and clean yet restrained," is a phrase that aptly describes this new mixed-use building in Chicago's Bucktown neighborhood. Eleven condominium units are located on three floors over ground-floor retail and below-grade indoor parking to create a strong, dynamic solution for this urban infill site. The building fills out the site to the sidewalk edge, lending Armitage/Leavitt a muscular city persona.

The simplicity of the building's design is evident in both the exterior as well as the highly organized typical floor plan. Vertically proportioned windows and a roofline that suggests a cornice reference the neighborhood's Victorian context while simultaneously creating a dramatic Modern design statement.

Hot-dipped galvanized steel used in lieu of historical limestone accents the planar masonry walls with their unusually deep-set windows, cut-out corner, and large retail show windows. The window lintels express the contemporary nature of the building's construction. Brick walls with knife-edge detailing suggest the building as a machine-made object.

The symmetrically organized plan provides four corner units per floor, each with the ideal split bedroom layout with corner living/dining spaces maximizing views. Units on two floors at the building's corner enjoy balconies that overlook the vibrant local scene. Durable yet elegant, the lobby utilizes plastic laminate wall surfacing along with ceramic tile in both matte and gloss finishes to provide an interplay between walls, floors, and openings. This arrangement of simple details, and a clear expression of the plan through the exterior, provides this building with a distinctive and dynamic presence in its neighborhood.

opposite   Shadowlines articulate building façade
right   Corner is occupied by balconies
below   Building as it meets its urban corner

below   Context of building's Bucktown neighborhood
opposite left   Detail of building as it addresses the corner
opposite right   Lobby is spare yet elegant in its detailing
photography   Pappageorge/Haymes

5th Street

Santa Monica, California
Koning Eizenberg Architecture

Family Housing

This project comprises 32 units of affordable family housing for the Community Corporation of Santa Monica. Twenty-two units are three-bedroom, two-level townhouses located at ground level. The third level provides two- and four-bedroom units, half of which are fitted for full disabled access. Units use cross-ventilation (there is no air-conditioning) and are arranged around two major communal spaces, a walk-street and a courtyard. The laundry and a small play area are located in the courtyard allowing parents to attend to chores while their children play.

Surprisingly, the key to releasing the potential of the site was the strategy to accommodate disabled access units on the third level rather than the ground level. Seemingly counterintuitive, this strategy made sense for many reasons. Because parking could only be provided underground, elevator access was required whether disabled access units were located on grade or an upper floor.

If two-level townhouse units were located on-grade, their small footprint would maximize the number of units that could be provided with on-grade garden courtyards thereby taking advantage of the large required side yard setbacks to create domestic amenity. A two-story townhouse with flats above required only one upper level walkway rather than two. This saved money, enhanced privacy, and permitted the architect freer play with the vertical scale of outdoor spaces.

The footprint of the third-level flats was significantly smaller than the levels below, allowing for large outside decks and a freer hand in form making that takes its lead from the adjacent lozenge-shaped bank building.

The result is a rather unconventional configuration that generates a new prototype for affordable family housing, introducing vitality through carefully organized social spaces, theatrical scale and color, and high-flying bridges.

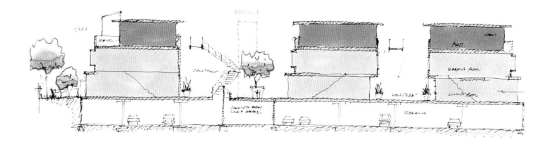

opposite top left   Color lends life to public spaces
opposite top right   Public spaces with bridges above
opposite bottom   Tower marks the center of complex
left   Units are light-filled
below left   Three-bedroom townhouse: ground floor plan
below right   Second floor plan
photography   Grant Mudford

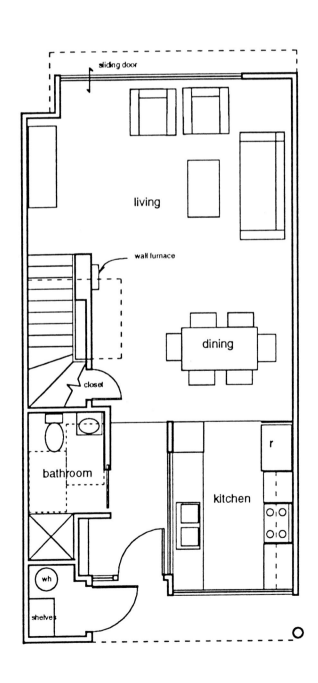

sliding door

living

wall furnace

dining

closet

bathroom

kitchen

r

wh

shelves

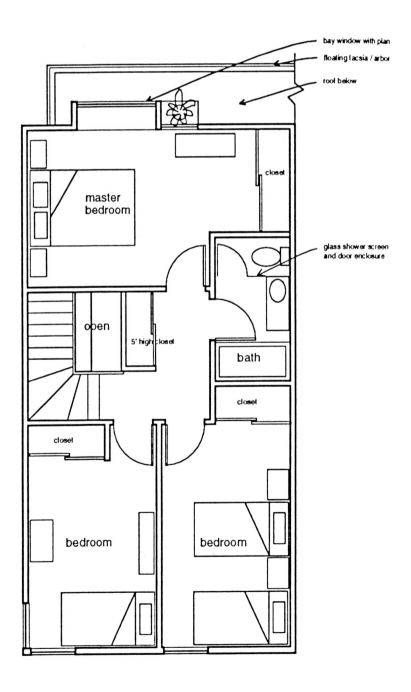

bay window with plan

floating fascia / arbor

roof below

master bedroom

closet

glass shower screen and door enclosure

open

5' high closet

bath

closet

closet

bedroom

bedroom

185

Johnson Street

Portland, Oregon
Mithun Architects

Townhomes

Located on the former Burlington Northern switching yards site in Portland's Pearl District, a historic warehouse quarter north of downtown, the Johnson Street Townhomes are designed to complement the scale and texture of the neighborhood's broad-shouldered, industrial architectural heritage. The three-story, 13-unit townhouse project offers an alternative to the Pearl District's single-story flats. With private courtyards and spacious units (ranging from 1,800 to 2,800 square feet), the townhomes are very much like single-family homes, yet feature roof-top balconies with city views, a live/work option in six of the units, and a strong street-level presence. The scale and design of the townhomes also disguise the high density of 26 units to the acre.

As a new urban infill community, the design challenge was to create a project that blends with the neighborhood and promotes a strong pedestrian link to the street. The Johnson Street project takes advantage of the industrial character inherent in the Pearl District. The exterior masonry blends with the existing warehouse buildings while the building's geometry exhibits an abstract interpretation of the warehouse aesthetic. The value of creating a sense of place while adding to the vibrancy of this emerging neighborhood is emphasized in all the design elements.

The street-level presence contributes to an interactive pedestrian experience, linking the townhouses to the nearby galleries, shops, and restaurants. Drawing on Portland's smart growth initiatives, Johnson Street Townhomes dovetail into the notion of providing more urban housing and live/work options in revitalized neighborhoods to attract new residents back to the city.

left Back of units face mews
opposite top Site plan
opposite middle top Alley elevation
opposite middle bottom Johnson Street elevation
opposite bottom left Units as they face the street
opposite bottom right Planters provide street buffers

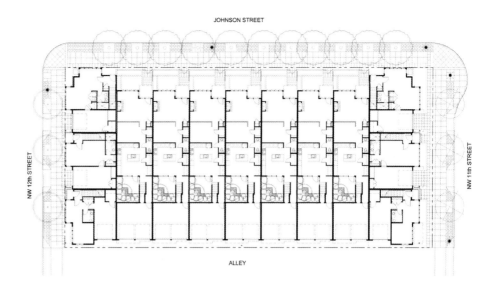

JOHNSON STREET

NW 12th STREET

NW 11th STREET

ALLEY

left top   Low walls allow uninterrupted views
left middle   Natural daylighting graces kitchen
left bottom   Interiors stress flow of space
below   Side elevation
opposite top   Decks are found on second level
opposite bottom left   Unit A, first floor plan
opposite bottom middle   Unit A, second floor plan
opposite bottom right   Unit A, third floor plan
photography   Eckert & Eckert

Tate Mason

Seattle, Washington
GGLO Architecture | House

Located in Seattle's historic First Hill community, this building is oriented to the southwest and wraps around the courtyard to maximize views and allow natural light in core areas. The 4,088-square-foot courtyard, built above street level for added privacy and security, has a patio area, benches, and gardening area for residents.

The lobby is adjacent to a spacious communal living room that opens onto the courtyard for indoor/outdoor use. The 97 studios and one-bedroom apartments share a sitting nook that overlooks the courtyard on each of the four floors. Details and massing of the Art Deco-inspired façade reinforce the urban character of this site, and complement the quality and scale of nearby buildings. Located in a central neighborhood near hospitals, medical facilities, downtown, shopping, and restaurants, the residents have easy access to these services.

The need for a new low-income senior housing project arose from the demolition of an existing housing project in downtown Seattle to make room for the city's convention center expansion. The Washington State Convention & Trade Center gave the developer a capital contribution for the replacement of the existing building. Part of the development agreement required the new project to be within a two-thirds-mile radius of the convention center so that disruption and inconvenience to existing residents would be minimal. Walking distance for residents is reduced through vertical access to units via multiple elevators and locating common rooms on the first level.

Although the site was zoned high-rise residential, the decision was deliberately made to keep the scale and height of the building in harmony with surrounding buildings and structures. Construction of the building required working around large trees, which were saved to keep the residential and historic character of the neighborhood. Tiles designed by local artists were used as an exterior design feature.

left top   Architectural details create added interest
left bottom   A projected enclave in the city
opposite top   Ramp access to main entry
opposite middle   Site plan
opposite bottom left   Entry to the complex
opposite bottom right   Tate Mason's variegated street façade

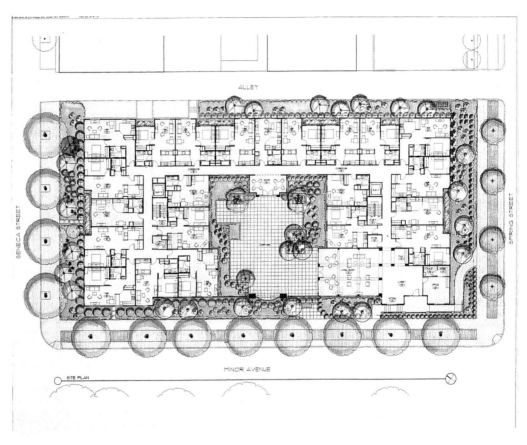

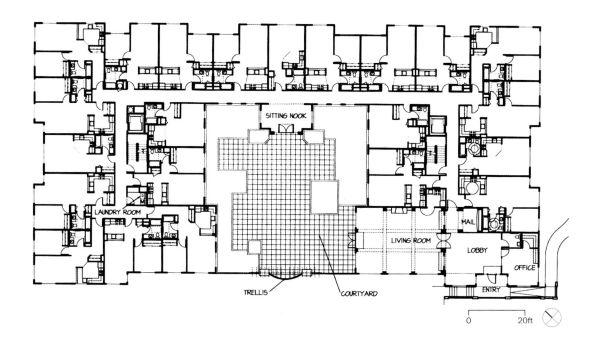

SITTING NOOK

LAUNDRY ROOM

LIVING ROOM

MAIL

LOBBY

OFFICE

ENTRY

TRELLIS

COURTYARD

0   20ft

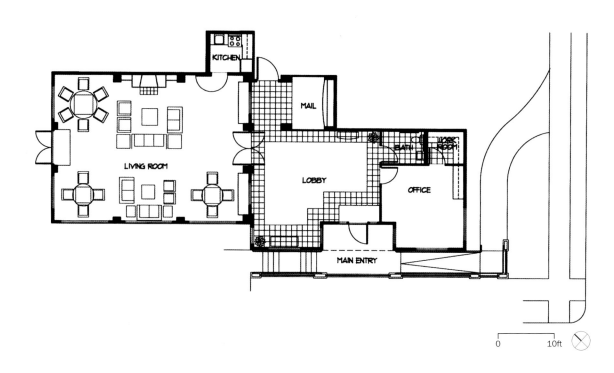

KITCHEN

MAIL

LIVING ROOM

LOBBY

BATH

OFFICE

MAIN ENTRY

0   10ft

opposite top   Courtyard space for residents' use
opposite middle   Ground floor plan
opposite bottom   Detail plan of common spaces
right top   Communal living room opens onto courtyard
right bottom   Communal living room has light interior
photography   Eduardo Calderon

The Siena

New York, New York
Hardy Holzman Pfeiffer Associates

The creation of this 31-story residential building was part of a strategy for the restoration of a New York City and National Register landmark church, St. Jean Baptiste Eglise. By purchasing air rights from the church and transferring them to the adjacent development parcel, the developer made critical funds available to an ongoing program of restoration and maintenance.

The new tower, designed to harmonize with the architectural style of the church and the rectory, is set back above the base to correspond to the massing of these two buildings. The lower portion of the building is constructed of granite and cast stone to harmonize with the limestone and granite used in the façade of the church and the rectory. This base is built to the street line to maintain the street wall established by the church, and the height of the cast-stone base matches that of the church.

The building's entrance is a correctly proportioned Doric door that emphasizes the building's classical context. At the same time, it expresses its individuality by distancing itself from its Corinthian neighbor. The tower is set back above the base to correspond to the massing of the church and the rectory.

Above the base, five colors of brick—alabaster, buff, light rose, dark red and plum—clad the building. The design is a play of verticals and horizontals, with the horizontals corresponding to the cornices of the church and verticals formed by the various faceted towers that compose the façade, recalling those on the church. The building's design incorporates a number of setbacks that allow small design details, such as windows and turrets, to read more clearly and allow tenants to see the city in unexpected ways.

The project houses 153,000 square feet of residential space and 13,000 square feet of commercial space. The 73 condominium apartments range from one-bedroom to five-bedroom triplexes.

right Tower architecture takes cues from church nearby
photography Cervin Robinson
opposite top Site plan
opposite bottom left Tower is a landmark in the neighborhood
photography Chris Lovi
opposite bottom right Building picks up fenestration and scale from church
photography Cervin Robinson

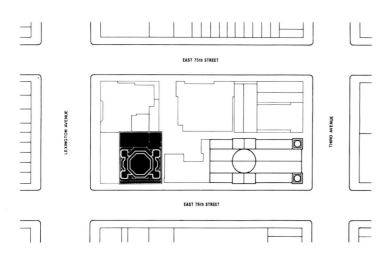

EAST 75th STREET

LEXINGTON AVENUE

THIRD AVENUE

EAST 76th STREET

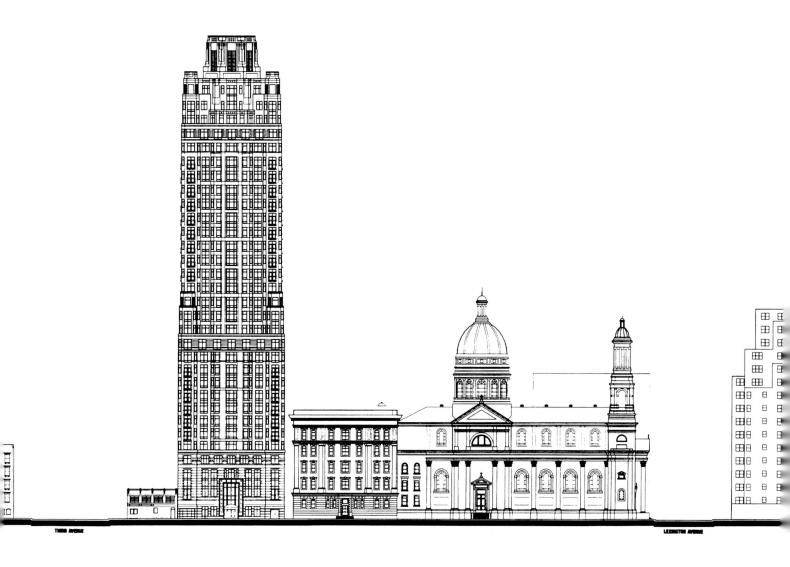

THIRD AVENUE   LEXINGTON AVENUE

opposite top — 76th Street elevation
opposite bottom — Tower has a solid base at street level
photography — Cervin Robinson
below — Imposing entry to residential tower
photography — Chris Lovi

Mockingbird

Station

Mockingbird Station, the center of Dallas' Southern Methodist University district, provides a pedestrian-scaled urban village where residents enjoy a stress-free way to access the greater Dallas community. The 10-acre multi-use transit-oriented development integrates housing, offices, shopping and entertainment with automobile, pedestrian, bicycle and public mass transit. This project is a worthy example of how new neighborhoods can be revived and created from buildings that have served one life and are ready to accommodate a new generation of uses.

A model for adaptive reuse, Mockingbird Station incorporates and extends existing warehouse and office buildings by adding more than 90 shops and restaurants, an eight-screen film center and café, a Virgin Megastore, and office space, along with 216 loft apartments and 1,600 parking spaces (most of them located underground).

Mockingbird offers a distinctive living environment amid the pulse of this urban neighborhood. The loft units surmount a warehouse building. From this vantage point, residents can enjoy views of the surrounding area. The light and airy units themselves exhibit a clean, sophisticated loft aesthetic, with exposed roof structures, warm natural materials, large expanses of glass, steel stairs to mezzanine level spaces, elegantly detailed kitchens, and exposed ductwork. Units also boast fireplaces, exposed concrete structural frames, and double-height living spaces.

Overall, the project's architecture is inspired by train station designs from an earlier era of rail travel, with a twist toward a modern aesthetic in materials and detailing. Thoughtfully orchestrated urban design assures a variety of comfortably scaled and detail-rich outdoor space.

Highlands Gardens-
Klahanie

Issaquah, Washington
Pyatok Architects

This project is the result of a joint partnership between two non-profit developers for low and very low-income households. The four-acre site is located in an upscale neighborhood of Issaquah, Washington on a moderately sloping site. The program called for 51 rental townhomes, a community building, laundry facilities, and play areas for children. Special design considerations were made to acknowledge the needs of large, often extended families of the Southeast Asian immigrant population, which has settled in the area over the last several years.

The project offers a mix of three-, four-, and five-bedroom units along with one- and two-bedroom units. The dining area in the four- and five-bedroom units is sized for extended family gatherings. Another feature is the "swing bedroom," which allows for some adjoining units to shrink or grow as needed.

Parking is located at the perimeter of the site, with housing and communal facilities at the center linked with pedestrian pathways. The Community Center has both indoor and outdoor meeting spaces, and includes play areas and community gardens. A large barbecue pit used throughout the year for various cultural events is also centrally located. A community garden set aside for resident use is located at the edge of the community. The entire project is accessible despite the fact that it includes a number of level changes.

Because several of the Southeast Asian residents came from mountainous regions, the housing's roof shapes were designed to symbolize both the local mountains and those of the residents' homelands. At the corner entries to each court and at the midpoint court entries the porches are topped with pyramidal hipped roofs, which in turn are clad in white roof shingles.

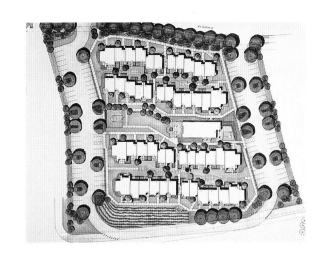

opposite left   Porches feature detailed columns and benches
opposite right   Pyramid roof elements anchor corners
top   Site plan
above   Development follows natural terrain of site
left   Scale of development is comfortably domestic

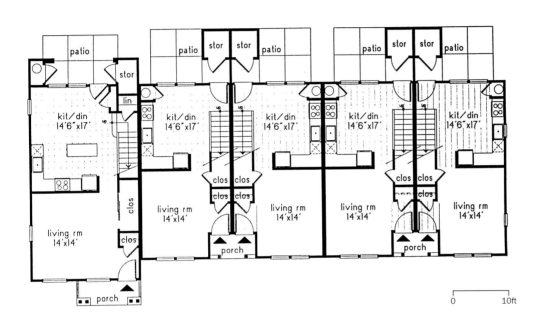

patio | stor | stor | patio | patio | stor | stor | patio

stor

lin

kit/din
14'6"x17'

kit/din
14'6"x17'

kit/din
14'6"x17'

kit/din
14'6"x17'

kit/din
14'6"x17'

clos

clos

living rm
14'x14'

clos | clos

clos | clos

living rm
14'x14'

living rm
14'x14'

living rm
14'x14'

clos | clos

clos | clos

living rm
14'x14'

clos

porch

porch

porch

0   10ft

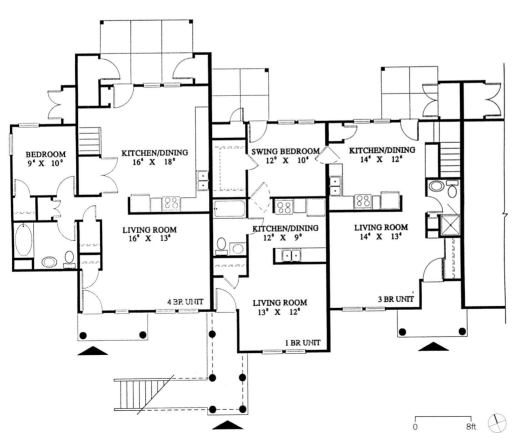

BEDROOM
9' X 10'

KITCHEN/DINING
16' X 18'

SWING BEDROOM
12' X 10'

KITCHEN/DINING
14' X 12'

LIVING ROOM
16' X 13'

KITCHEN/DINING
12' X 9'

LIVING ROOM
14' X 13'

4 BR UNIT

LIVING ROOM
13' X 12'

3 BR UNIT

1 BR UNIT

0   8ft

INDEX

ACKNOWLEDGMENTS

Many people were involved in the creation of this book. Thanks are extended to the architects and designers who agreed to have their projects published (and to the developers and non-profit organizations that had the foresight to build them). Special gratitude is expressed to the photographers who generously allowed use of their photographs. Michael Pyatok's Introduction is an invaluable addition to this book for which I am deeply grateful. Finally, thanks to Alessina Brooks and Paul Latham of The Images Publishing Group and its staff for their support of this publication, and for bringing it to fruition.